craft tree

Everyday Totes

Compiled By **Barbara Delaney**

INTERWEAVE
interweave.com

Interweave grants permission to photocopy the templates in this publication for personal use.

The projects in this collection were originally published in other Interweave publications, including 101 Patchwork, Modern Patchwork, Quilt Scene, Quilting Arts, *and* Stitch *magazines and* 'QATV.' *Some have been altered to update information and/or conform to space limitations.*

Interweave Press LLC
A division of F+W Media, Inc
201 East Fourth Street
Loveland, CO 80537
interweave.com

Manufactured in the United States by Versa Press

ISBN 978-1-59668-774-5 (pbk.)

Table of Contents

Materials

—Ink-jet cotton sheets (EQ Printables Cotton, Jacquard Ink-jet Printing Cotton, etc.) for ink-jet collage for the bag flap

—½ yd (46 cm) Fabric A (see Note): cotton fabric for outer bag body and shoulder strap

—½ yd (46 cm) or 1 fat quarter Fabric B (see Note): cotton fabric for bag and flap lining

—½ yd (46 cm) Pellon Fusible Fleece 987F (This is what I prefer; the fusible is not necessary, but it's easier to handle fused components when stitching.)

—Thread for machine stitching and quilting

—Computer

—Scanner

—Ink-jet printer

—Sewing machine

—Steam iron

---

note

* You can use assorted fabrics, as I did; the strap requires a 42" (106.5 cm) fabric length; otherwise, several fat quarters will provide variety.

Make Your Ink-jet Collage Print

1 Choose or design a collage to use in your 7½" (19 cm) square. You can scan a traditional cut-and-paste paper collage to print or, if you're familiar with Photoshop or similar computer art programs, you can scan various vintage images from your collection into your computer to layer into a digital collage, as I have done. If you don't collect antique prints, most bookstores sell clip art books with CDs that offer many beautiful vintage images you can use for your digital or paper compositions.

Note: In sewing, you will lose the outer ¼" (6 mm) of your collage image for the seam allowance all around, so make sure no critical artistic elements fall within the outer ¼" (6 mm) of your collage image. Note my use of striped fabric border strips

INK-JET FABRIC COLLAGE
Mini Messenger Bag
by LuAnne Hedblom

I enjoy making bags that feature my own nature-themed collages, which combine antique flower or bird images with vintage text. I print my collages on ink-jet cotton sheets and combine these prints with commercial cotton fabrics for a one-of-a-kind handmade gift.

The mini messenger bag featured here is a quick and simple project. However, you may need to print your ink-jet collage a day ahead of sewing to allow sufficient time for the ink to dry, depending on which type of ink-jet cotton sheet you use.

around the edges of the bag's collage; text, plain, or textured backgrounds around the border work well, too, to help keep your design intact without worrying about where the seam line falls.

2 Print your collage on an ink-jet cotton sheet, following the manufacturer's instructions. For printing, I usually increase the image contrast and saturation, because fabric absorbs more ink than paper would. Also, I have found that on my Epson C120 printer, using the "best photo" and "premium matte paper" print settings works best for me.

Tip

Ink-jet cotton sheets are a bit costly, so to avoid waste, first test print your image (on matte cardstock if possible) at these "best" settings to see how it looks. With my printer, if the card stock print seems a tiny bit bright, the fabric version will likely be right.

3 Allow the sheet to dry according to the product directions.

4 Rinse the sheet well to assure all excess ink is removed. Once it's dry, I always press it on the wrong side at the cotton/full steam setting to make sure that any shrinkage occurs before I cut my 7½" (19 cm) square for the bag flap.

Note: It's best to follow the manufacturer's instructions for rinsing, drying, and ironing your printed image.

Sewing the Bag

5 When your ink-jet collage print is dry, ironed, and ready to use, cut out all your pattern pieces:

Bag body: Cut 2 pieces 7½" × 10½" (19 × 26.5 cm) each of Fabric A, Fabric B, and fusible fleece.

Bag flap: Cut 1 piece 7½" × 7½" (19 × 19 cm) each of ink-jet collage, Fabric B, and fusible fleece.

Strap: Cut 1 piece 4½" × 42" (11.5 × 106.5 cm) of Fabric A. Cut 1 piece 2¼" × 42" (5.5 × 106.5 cm) of fusible fleece.

Tip

If your ink-jet collage image on the fabric has shrunk a bit to slightly less than a 7½" (19 cm) square, don't panic. Just be sure to leave enough plain fabric around the image equally, then cut the full 7½" (19 cm) square with your image centered.

6 Following the product instructions, fuse the fleece pieces to the wrong side of the ink-jet print flap and the 2 Fabric A main bag pieces. Set the bag pieces aside.

Note: Fusible fleece is not supposed to shrink. However, just before I fuse it in place, I hold the steam iron about ½" (1.3 cm) above the surface and steam well over the entire surface of the piece I'm about to fuse. It only takes a few extra seconds and ensures that any miniscule potential shrinkage occurs before I fuse the fleece to my fabric piece. I think it gives a nicer finish to my fused pieces.

7 Put a pin in the top edge of your fused ink-jet collage to temporarily mark it as the top. Place the Fabric B flap lining and the ink-jet collage flap right sides together; they should be the same size. Using a ¼" (6 mm) seam allowance, sew down one side, across the bottom, and up the other side. Leave the top edge open, remove your marking pin, and turn the flap right-side out, being careful your corners are fully turned and crisp.

Note: Your flap should now be about 7" (18 cm) wide by 7¼" (18.5 cm) long, with raw edges at the top.

8 Press the flap, making sure the edges are all even and straight. With the right-side up, topstitch ¼"–½" (6 mm–1.3 cm) from the side and bottom edges. Finally, stitch across the top very close to the raw edge, just to keep all the layers together neatly.

9 Machine quilt the 2 Fabric A main bag pieces as desired. Straight stitching is easy and it always looks good. For quilting guidelines, I use tailor's chalk to draw a line down the center of the pieces lengthwise, and then I draw a line every 1" (2.5 cm) or so to either side, but no closer than ¾" (2 cm) to the edges. After stitching the quilting lines, brush away any remaining chalk.

Tip

For a subtle effect, choose a matching quilting thread. For fun, choose a contrasting color, taking your thread color cues from your ink-jet collage. Changing threads on different fabrics is a good way to add interest.

10 Place the 2 quilted main bag pieces right sides together and sew with a ¼" (6 mm) seam allowance: down 1 long side, across the bottom, and up the other long side, leaving the top open. Turn right-side out, corners crisp, edges straight and even, and press.

11 Center the 2¼" (5.5 cm) strip of fusible fleece on the wrong side of the Fabric A strap piece and fuse it in place. Fold the unfused fabric on either side of the fleece strip in, so the lengthwise edges meet in the center, right-sides up and press. (The fleece is now completely enclosed by fabric.) Fold the strap in half lengthwise, pin the folded edges together as needed to secure, and stitch ¼" (6 mm) from the edge all the way along both long edges. Press.

12 Match each raw end of the strap with the raw top edge of 1 side of the Fabric A bag back, right sides together and about ¼" (6 mm) away from the side seams. (If you've used assorted fabrics, this is the intended back.) Take time to double-check to make sure the strap is not twisted before you stitch. Stitch close to the raw edge to secure, taking care to stitch through only 1 layer of the bag.

13 Match the raw edge of the collage bag flap with the raw edge of Fabric A bag, right sides together, on top of the strap layer you've just sewn. Pin as needed to secure, and stitch all the way across the top, close

to the raw edge, again stitching through only 1 layer of the bag. Set aside.

Note: The flap, lining-side out, should now cover the strap and should just barely meet each side seam of the bag.

14 On 1 short end of each Fabric B lining piece, press a generous ¼" (6 mm) toward the back side, but do not sew along the pressed edge yet. Place both Fabric B bag lining pieces right sides together, with the pressed-under ends matching. Sew a ¼" (6 mm) seam along each long edge.

15 Slip the inside-out Fabric B lining tube up over the bag/strap/flap assembly, so the raw top edges match and the side seams align. The right side of the lining should be facing the right side of the bag underneath on 1 side, and the flap lining on the other side. Pin as needed to secure the raw edges. Sew with a ¼" (6 mm) seam allowance all the way around this top edge of the bag/lining.

16 Pull the lining up over the top of the bag, turning the lining right-side out, but keep the bag flap and strap with the Fabric A bag section for now. Flatten the lining section, with seams to each side, and stitch the previously pressed-under edges together, close to the edge.

> **Tip**
>
> If you wish, take a moment now to sign your name on the lining with a fine permanent marker.

17 Press the lining section and then tuck it neatly all the way down inside the bag. The seam that joins the outer bag to the lining should form the top edge of the bag now. Take care to press the top of the bag so that this top edge is neat and even, and pin as needed to secure. Then, with the flap and strap extended above the bag body, right-sides out, topstitch around the top edge of the bag body, ¼" (6 mm) below the top edge/flap seam.

18 Touch up the outer bag with a steam iron, taking care to flatten any bulk at the top of each side seam. The flap should fall down over the outer bag body to form the front of the bag, proudly displaying your beautiful ink-jet collage. ✑

See more of **LUANNE HEDBLOM'S** work at invisiblewoman.typepad.com.

For a nice extra touch, tuck a small journal or nature guide inside the bag. I glued the paper version of my bird collage to the cover of this moleskin journal.

Painted Grocery Tote
by Valori Wells

Fancy this: a painted canvas and fabric appliqué grocery tote! With this unique piece on your arm, you're sure to be a big hit at the market or with your sewing group. This grocery tote is created by painting on canvas and by adding bits of your favorite fabrics, resulting in a unique carryall for your projects, groceries, and any other items you choose.

Materials
—54" (137 cm) wide canvas, 1½–2 yd (137–183 cm) (This is more than you will need but will allow you to paint a large area and get enough of the painting into the bag.)

—Fabric or plastic to protect your work surface

—45" (114.5 cm) wide lining fabric, 1 yd (91.5 cm)

—Scraps of favorite fabrics for appliqué

—Acrylic paint or textile paint to match your scrap fabric

—Paintbrushes (Choose sizes that will work for your design.)

—Thread to match your paint

Paint Your Fabric

1 Secure the canvas to a wall or place it on the floor. Make sure you have some fabric or plastic under the canvas in case the paint goes through the fabric.

2 Either draw the design with a pencil first or free-form paint. You can use motifs from your favorite fabrics as inspiration for the painting. I used the dahlia and leaf design from one of the fabrics in my "Nest" collection (by FreeSpirit) as inspiration (**figure 1**).

Cut and Prepare

3 Once your painted canvas is dry, line up the selvages and cut 1 strip that is 5" (12.5 cm) wide, 1 strip that is 8" (20.5 cm) wide, and 1 strip that is 15" (38 cm) wide. From these strips, cut the front, back, sides, bottom, and handles, as follows:

—(2) 15" × 15" (38 × 38 cm) squares (front and back of bag)

—(3) 8" × 15" (20.5 × 38 cm) strips (sides and bottom of bag)

—(2) 5" × 26" (12.5 × 66 cm) strips (handles)

Note: You can also fussy cut the pieces of your bag; just make sure you cut the strips that are 5" × 26" (12.5 × 66 cm) for the handles.

4 Cut the following pieces from your lining fabric:

—(2) 15" × 15" (38 × 38 cm) squares (front and back lining)

—(3) 8" × 15" strips (20.5 × 38 cm) (sides and bottom lining)

FIGURE 1

FIGURE 2

FIGURE 3

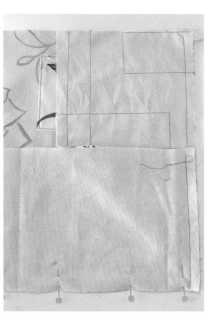

FIGURE 4

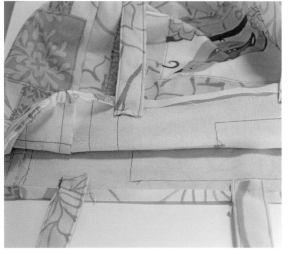

FIGURE 5

5 Cut squares and rectangles from your favorite fabrics and arrange them on the body of your bag until you are satisfied with their placement, then pin them in place **(figure 2)**. Topstitch approximately ⅛" (3 mm) from the edge around the perimeter of each fabric piece.

Note: If you don't want raw edges, turn the fabric pieces under ⅛"–¼" (3–6 mm), press, and then pin them onto the canvas.

6 To make the handles, fold 1 of the 5" × 26" (12.5 × 66 cm) strips in half lengthwise, wrong sides facing, and press. Unfold the strip, then fold the long raw edges to the center fold and press. Fold the strip in half so that the raw edges are inside the folded handle. Topstitch along both long edges of the handle. Repeat for the second 5" × 26" (12.5 × 66 cm) strip.

Construct the Bag Body

Note: All seam allowances are ½" (1.3 cm).

7 With right sides facing, stitch together 1 bottom piece and 1 side piece along their 8" (20.5 cm) sides, starting and stopping ½" (1.3 cm) from the ends. (If the design on the side of your bag is directional, make sure you are sewing the bottom edge of the side to the bottom piece.) Stitch the other side piece to the bottom piece in the same way so that you have 1 long side-bottom unit.

8 Pin the front of the bag to 1 of the sides in the side-bottom unit with right sides facing. Stitch the side and front together, starting from the top and ending ½" (1.3 cm) from the bottom. Backstitch to secure your stitches **(figure 3)**.

9 Fold the side-bottom unit so that the long side of the bottom piece lines up with the bottom of the bag front, with right sides facing, and pin these pieces together **(figure 4)**. Stitch, starting and stopping ½" (1.3 cm) from the ends, and backstitching to secure your stitches.

10 Fold the side-bottom unit so that the unstitched side piece lines up with the other side of the front, and pin. Stitch ½" (1.3 cm) from the bottom and all the way to the top.

11 Repeat Steps 2–4 with the other side of the side-bottom unit and the back of the bag.

12 Repeat Steps 1–5 with the lining fabric.

Final Assembly

13 Fold and press ½" (1.3 cm) around the top edge of the bag, pressing toward the bag interior. Repeat with the lining. Press the side seams of the bag toward the front and back pieces. Press the side seams of the lining toward the sides; this will nest the seams when you are stitching the bag together.

14 To place the handles, measure 2½" (6.5 cm) in from 1 of the side seams and 1" (2.5 cm) down from the top edge. Pin 1 end of 1 handle in place. Repeat this measuring and pinning on the same side of the bag with the other end of the handle. Turn the bag to the other side and pin the other handle in the same way **(figure 5)**.

15 Turn the bag right-side out and the lining wrong-side out. Insert the lining into the bag so that the wrong sides of the lining and bag are touching.

16 Pin the top edges of the bag and lining together (the ends of the handles will be inside the 2 layers), then topstitch around the top edge to secure the lining to the bag.

17 Press your bag and go shopping! ✑

VALORI WELLS is the author of *Simple Start Stunning Finish* and the co-owner of The Stitchin' Post in Sisters, Oregon. Visit her website at valoriwells .com.

Checkerboard Bag
by Ayumi Takahashi

Mix several shades of linen to create this quilted patchwork bag inspired by wooden checkerboards. Its roomy design, soft flannel lining, and inside pocket will ensure it carries everything you need. Machine embroidery accents the patchwork and fabric handles.

Materials

—½ yd (46 cm) each of 2 different colors of 45" (114.5 cm) wide linen for patchwork and handles (A and B; shown: 2 different shades of natural linen)

—½ yd (46 cm) each of 2 different colors of 45" (114.5 cm) wide linen for patchwork, circle appliqué, and shell base (C and D; shown: 2 different shades of dark brown)

—¼ yd (23 cm) each of 2 different 45" (114.5 cm) wide linen prints for circle appliqué (E and F; shown: 2 different natural linen prints)

—8" (20.5 cm) square scrap of linen plaid for circle appliqué (G; shown: natural linen plaid)

—⅛ yd (11.5 cm) of 45" (114.5 cm) wide print cotton for lining handles (H; shown: brown polka dot)

—¾ yd (68.5 cm) of 45" (114.5 cm) wide flannel for lining (I; shown: tan)

—5½" × 10½" (14 × 26.5 cm) piece of print cotton for pocket (J; shown: white polka dot)

—¾ yd (68.5 cm) of cotton batting (Recommended: Warm and Natural cotton batting)

—1 yd (91.5 cm) of paper-backed fusible web

—5" (12.5 cm) square of lightweight fusible interfacing

—Cotton sewing thread to match fabrics A/B

—Cotton sewing thread to match fabrics C/D

—Cotton sewing thread to match flannel

—2" (5 cm) of ⅝" (1.5 cm) wide ribbon (optional)

—Handsewing needle

—Quilt-basting spray

—Fabric marking pencil

—Walking foot and quilting guide (optional) for sewing machine

—Checkerboard Bag templates on page 12

Finished Size
About 15" high without handles × 20" wide at the top (38 × 51 cm); 12" (30.5 cm) wide at the bottom

notes

✻ All seam allowances are ¼" (6 mm) unless otherwise noted.

✻ For explanations of terms and techniques see Sewing Basics.

Cut the Fabric

1 Cut the following pieces as directed; you may want to label pieces on the wrong side with a fabric pencil or use tape for temporary labels to avoid confusion as you put the bag together.

From fabric A:

—Sixteen 3½" (9 cm) squares for patchwork

—Two 2¼" × 25" (5.5 × 63.5 cm) strips for Shell Handles

From fabric B:

—Nineteen 3½" (9 cm) squares for patchwork

From fabric C:

—Fifteen 3½" (9 cm) squares for patchwork

—One 7" × 14" (18 × 35.5 cm) piece for Shell Base

—Eighteen 3" (7.5 cm) squares for Circle Appliqués

From fabric D:

—Twenty 3½" (9 cm) squares for patchwork

—Seventeen 3" (7.5 cm) squares for Circle Appliqués

From fabric E:

—Nine 3" (7.5 cm) squares for Circle Appliqués

From fabric F:

—Ten 3" (7.5 cm) squares for Circle Appliqués

From fabric G:

—Six Circle Appliqués (following method described in Step 6)

From fabric H:

—Two 2¼" × 25" (5.5 × 63.5 cm) strips for Lining Handles

From fabric I:

—Two 20¾" × 15¼" (52.5 × 38.5 cm) pieces for Lining

—One Lining Base using Shell/ Lining Base pattern

From the cotton batting:

—Two 25½" × 19½" (65 × 49.5 cm) pieces for Shell Interlining

—Two 11" × 18" (28 × 45.5 cm) pieces for Shell Base Interlining

Assemble the Shell

2 Using the linen 3½" (9 cm) squares (fabrics A, B, C, and D), create two 7 × 5 patchwork panels in a checkered pattern. Begin by placing a light and a dark linen square right sides together and seaming along one side. Add five more patches, alternating dark and light squares, to make a 7-patch row. Repeat to make nine more 7-patch rows, then join the rows to make 2 panels of 5 rows each.

3 Spray the wrong side of each patchwork panel with quilt-basting spray and center it right-side up on one of the Shell Interlining batting pieces.

4 Machine quilt each panel by sewing a square about 1⁄16" (2 mm) inside the patchwork seams on each of the square patches, using thread that matches the patch and a walking foot if desired. Along the outer edges of the patchwork, the quilted squares should be about 5⁄16" (8 mm) from the raw edges so they aren't obscured by seams sewn later.

5 Using the provided Circle Appliqué template, draw 60 circles on the paper side of the fusible web, leaving 1" (2.5 cm) between circles.

6 Rough cut these circles, leaving a small extra margin of fusible web around each, then fuse one to the wrong side of each 3" (7.5 cm) square (cut from fabrics C, D, E, and F). Cut out the circles along the drawn lines on the fusible web, peel off the paper backing, and fuse each circle onto a square patch in the patchwork panels, placing light-colored circles on dark square patches and dark circles on light squares. (There will be 5 patches without a circle on each side of the bag, so arrange your circles as desired or refer to the photo on page 9 for the arrangement seen in the sample). This will now be referred to as the shell.

7 To secure the Circle Appliqués of fabrics C, D, E, F, and G to the shell, machine quilt around each Circle Appliqué using a zigzag stitch about ¹⁄₁₆–⅛" (2–3 mm) wide and 1 mm long (25 stitches per inch) with thread that matches the square patch under the circle, pivoting frequently with the needle in the square patch.

8 Place the patchwork panels right sides together (making sure the checkerboard pattern of the patchwork continues where the panels meet), pin, and sew the two short edges to make a tube. Set it aside.

9 Spray the wrong side of the fabric C Shell Base with quilt-basting spray and center it right-side up on one of the Shell Base Interlining batting pieces. Spray the remaining Shell Base Interlining batting piece and adhere it to the other side of the first batting piece. Using matching thread and a walking foot, machine quilt in a diagonal grid pattern with lines spaced about ½" (1.3 cm) apart. Use the edge of your presser foot or a quilting guide to keep the spacing of the lines even.

10 Use the provided Shell/Lining Base pattern to cut the Shell Base from the quilted piece completed in Step 9 and mark at the middle of each edge.

11 With right sides together, pin the Shell Base to the quilted Shell from Step 8, aligning the notches on the curved ends of the Shell Base with the side seams of the Shell and the notches on the straight edges of the Shell Base with the middle of each patchwork panel's bottom edge. Create ⅝" (1.5 cm) wide pleats to fit the Shell to the Shell Base by folding the square patch seams toward the center of each side. Pin each pleat to secure, adjusting the depth

of the pleats if necessary to fit the Shell Base **(figure 1)**. Sew the Shell and Shell Base together, being sure to catch the pleats in the stitching.

Assemble the Lining

12 Fold the fabric J Pocket in half widthwise, with right sides together.

13 Sew the raw edges together, leaving a 2" (5 cm) opening in one edge for turning.

14 Fuse the 5" (12.5 cm) square of lightweight fusible interfacing to one side of the Pocket. Turn the Pocket right-side out through the opening, folding in and finger pressing the seam allowances at the opening.

15 Pin this pocket to the right side of one fabric I Lining piece, with the folded edge on top about 2¼" (5.5 cm) from the upper long edge of the Lining piece and the pocket centered between the short edges of the Lining. Fold the ribbon in half widthwise and sandwich the raw ends between the pocket and the Lining at the right bottom edge (optional; see photo on page 12). Topstitch the sides and bottom edges of the pocket, reinforcing the ends of the stitching by sewing a small triangle of stitches near the top edge when starting and stopping.

16 Sew the two short edges of the two Lining pieces with right sides together to make a tube, leaving a 4½" (11.5 cm) opening at one side edge.

17 Pin the Lining Base to the lining tube with right sides together, aligning, pleating, and sewing as described in Step 11.

Make the Handles

18 Place one Shell Handle right sides together with one Lining Handle, aligning all edges. Pin and then sew together along one long (25" [63.5 cm]) edge. Open out the seamed handle pieces, press the seam allowances open, and then fold each long raw edge toward the wrong side so that the raw edges meet at the seams; press. Refold the handle along the seam, wrong sides together, and sew along the open long edge. Press flat. You now have a handle that is 1" (2.5 cm) wide. Repeat this entire step with the remaining Shell Handle and Lining Handle to make the second handle.

19 Using matching thread for both the top and the bobbin thread, topstitch along each long edge of the handles, ⅛" (3 mm) from the edge.

20 Using contrasting thread, straight stitch random zigzags from one long edge of each handle to the other long edge. Work from one end of the handle, zigzagging back and forth and pivoting with the needle in the fabric near the long edges, and when you reach the opposite end, turn the handle and zigzag randomly back over the handle again. Make several passes of zigzags this way to create the overlapped zigzag shown in the sample (see photo on page 9).

Finish

21 Place one handle on each side of the shell bag, right sides together, aligning the raw ends of the handle with the top raw edge of the shell bag and centering the handle with 3 square patches between the two handle ends **(figure 2)**. Machine baste the handle ends in place, ⅛" (3 mm) from the edge.

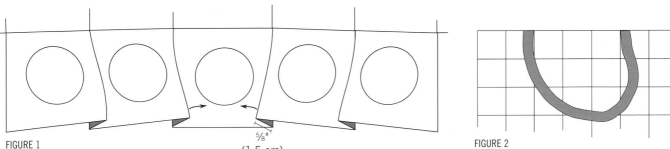

FIGURE 1

⅝"
(1.5 cm)

FIGURE 2

22 With the lining inside out, pull it up around the shell, aligning the side seams and the top raw edges. Make sure the handles are sandwiched in between; pin and then stitch together around the top edge. Carefully pull the shell through the opening in the side of the lining. Turn in the seam allowances at the opening and finger press, then handstitch closed with a slip stitch. Stuff the lining down inside the shell.

23 Topstitch around the top edge of the bag, ⅛" (3 mm) from the edge, being sure to keep the handles out of the way of the stitching. 🌿

AYUMI TAKAHASHI shares her craft projects and easy sewing tutorials on her blog, *Pink Penguin*, at ayumills .blogspot.com.

circle appliqué
This template is actual size

shell/lining base
cut 2 on fold as directed
Enlarge this template 115%

⌐ place on fold ⌐

Carpet Bag
by Linda Turner Griepentrog

Refashion a colorful woven throw rug into a sturdy market tote that folds flat for carrying, but opens wide to hold a day's worth of shopping fun. The pre-finished rug edges make this a quick-to-sew project.

Materials

—2' × 3' (61 cm × 91.5 cm) throw rug

—⅓ yd (30.5 cm) of coordinating lightweight cotton for insert cover

—5½" × 16" (14 cm × 40.5 cm) piece of acrylic for bag bottom support (change the dimensions if necessary to match rug variations; see Notes)

—Coordinating sewing thread

—Size 100/16 to 110/18 sewing machine needle

—32" (81.5 cm) leather purse handles

—Walking foot for sewing machine (optional)

—Hot glue gun and glue

Finished Size

17" wide × 15" high × 6" deep (43 cm × 38 cm × 15 cm). Tote size varies with original rug size.

---

notes

* All seam allowances are ½" (1.3 cm) unless otherwise noted.

* Depending on the rug weight, it may be necessary to slow the machine speed to avoid needle breakage, handstitch the thickest area, or take the rug to an upholstery shop for stitching.

* The acrylic sheet used for the sample was purchased at a home improvement store and cut to size with a circular saw. Most home improvement stores will cut the sheets for you, if requested.

* A walking foot will help keep the layers even as you sew.

Attach the Handles

1 Measure the short finished rug ends and mark the center point. Place a pin 3" (7.5 cm) from the center on each side and 5" (12.5 cm) below the finished edge; repeat on the other end of the rug.

2 Following the manufacturer's instructions, attach the handles to each side of the tote at the marked locations.

Construct the Tote

3 Fold the rug right sides together and stitch the side seams; press the seams open. Topstitch on both sides of the seam if desired to hold the seam allowances open. Pin-mark the bag bottom fold line.

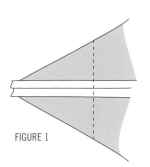

FIGURE 1

4 Fold the bag, right sides together, to match one seam line to the bottom fold line, forming a point. Measure 6" (15 cm) from the point along the seam line and draw a line perpendicular to the side seam. Stitch on the line, forming a triangular corner (**figure 1**). Repeat for the other lower corner. Turn the bag right-side out and smooth the corners into place.

Finish

5 Wrap the acrylic insert with fabric, turning under one long edge ¼" (6 mm) and lapping it over the other cut edge. Whipstitch to secure. Finish the ends as if wrapping a package, trimming the excess length and turning under the raw edges before whipstitching. Insert the covered support into the bag bottom, tucking it under the corner flaps, and attach with glue.

6 To shape the upper corners, measure and pin-mark the upper edge 3" (7.5 cm) from the side seams on the front and back. With wrong sides together, fold the bag at each pin and edgestitch the fold from the upper edge to ½" (1.3 cm) below the edge (the stitching will be visible on the outside of the bag). 🖉

LINDA TURNER GRIEPENTROG is the owner of G Wiz Creative Services in Bend, Oregon. She writes, edits and designs for a number of companies and leads sewing tours for the American Sewing Guild.

Ruffle Tote
by Carol Zentgraf

Think spring with a cheerful Ultrasuede tote in a fashion-forward color. Embellished with large ruffles and contrasting buttons, this roomy bag features a coordinating print lining with handy pockets.

Materials

- 1 yd (91.5 cm) of 46" (117 cm) wide Ultrasuede (Main; shown: bright yellow from Toray at ultrasuede.com) for shell
- ⅞ yd (80 cm) of 45" (114.5 cm) wide coordinating cotton print (Lining) for lining
- ½ yd (46 cm) sew-in interfacing
- Self-adhesive, double-stick basting tape (such as Wonder Tape)
- All-purpose sewing thread
- Removable fabric marker
- Two 1⅛" (29 mm) shank buttons (shown: JHB #80233)
- Two 1½" (38 mm) shank buttons (shown: JHB #80231)
- Pattern tracing cloth or paper
- Handsewing needle
- Ruffle Tote template on page 16

Finished Size

About 16" (40.5 cm) high × 18" (45.5 cm) wide without handle.

notes

* All seam allowances are ½" (1.3 cm) unless otherwise indicated.

* For explanations of terms and techniques, see Sewing Basics.

* Needles and pins will leave permanent holes in Ultrasuede. Avoid removing seams and keep all pins, if necessary, inside the seam allowances; use basting tape instead of pins where possible.

* Do not press Ultrasuede with an iron; finger-press seams and edges as needed and use topstitching to hold them in place as directed.

Cut Fabric

1 Trace the tote pattern onto the folded pattern tracing cloth or paper to make a complete shape. Cut out the pattern.

2 From Main, cut:
- 2 Bag Body pieces
- 5½" × 46" (14 × 117 cm) strip (bottom ruffle)
- 4½" × 46" (11.5 × 117 cm) strip (middle ruffle)
- 4½" × 39" (11.5 × 99 cm) strip (top ruffle)
- 2" × 24" (5 × 61 cm) strip (handle)

- 4" × 12" (10 × 30.5 cm) rectangle (closure strap)

3 From Lining, cut:
- 2 Bag Body pieces
- 11" (28 cm) square (pocket)

4 From interfacing, cut:
- 2 Bag Body pieces
- 1½" × 23" (3.8 × 58.5 cm) strip (handle)
- 3" × 11" (7.5 × 28 cm) rectangle (closure strap)

Assemble Tote Shell & Lining

5 To assemble the tote shell, baste (with basting tape) an interfacing piece to the wrong side of each Main Bag Body piece. Sew the darts and finger-press downward. Edgestitch close to each dart, through all the layers, and trim the excess fabric on the wrong side. Sew the front and back together along the sides, matching the darts. Turn right-side out.

6 For each ruffle strip, sew the short edges together with a ¼" (6 mm) seam. Finger-press the seam allowances open. Topstitch close to the seam on each side to hold the seam allowances in place. Sew a gathering stitch (to avoid extra needle holes in the faux suede, only one row of gathering stitches is used) ¼" (6 mm) from one edge of each 46" (117 cm) long ruffle strip (bottom and middle ruffles). Place the completed tote shell on a flat surface. Slip the bottom ruffle around the shell, placing the gathered edge 5" (12.5 cm) above the bottom edge, following the shape of the bag and positioning the seam at the center back. The lower edge of the ruffle will fall along the bag bottom seam. Secure the gathered edge to the tote with basting tape, then topstitch in place along the gathering stitch line. Repeat with the middle ruffle, arranging it so the lower edge overlaps the gathered edge of the bottom ruffle 1¼" (3.2 cm). To add the top ruffle, apply basting tape along one long edge and slip the ruffle over the shell. Remove the paper backing from the tape, evenly gather the edge by hand, and adhere it to the shell, with the gathered edge 2" (5 cm) below the bag's upper edge. The bottom edge will overlap the top of the middle ruffle. Topstitch the top ruffle in place, ¼" (6 mm) from the gathered upper edge of the ruffle.

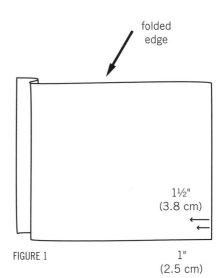

folded edge

1½" (3.8 cm)

FIGURE 1   1" (2.5 cm)

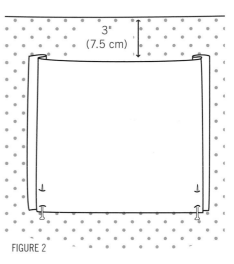

3" (7.5 cm)

FIGURE 2

7 Fold the cotton pocket square in half with right sides together. Sew the raw edges together, leaving an opening for turning. Trim the corners diagonally, turn right-side out, and press. Handstitch the opening closed with a slip stitch. Measure and mark 1" (2.5 cm) and 1½" (3.8 cm) from each corner on the long, stitched pocket edge. Fold the pocket on one 1½" (3.8 cm) mark and bring the fold to meet the nearby 1" (2.5 cm) mark, forming a small pleat (**figure 1**). Pin the pleat at the pocket's lower (stitched) edge to secure. Repeat to make a pleat near the second corner (refer to **figure 1**). Center the pocket on the right side of one Lining bag body piece, with the pocket's folded edge 3" (7.5 cm) from the bag body's upper raw edge (**figure 2**). Pin the upper corners of the pocket 9" (23 cm) apart to correspond to the pleats; the upper edge of the pocket will bow

Enlarge template 220%

Ruffle Tote
Bag Body
Cut 2 on fold from Main
Cut 2 on fold from Lining

place on fold

away from the lining. Edgestitch the side and bottom edges of the pocket to secure it to the lining, stitching through the pleats at the lower edge. To divide the pocket, topstitch a vertical line down the pocket, 3" (7.5 cm) from one short edge.

8 Follow Step 5 to sew the darts in the Lining bag body pieces, but do not edgestitch or trim the lining darts. Sew the Lining bag body pieces along the side edges, right sides together, matching the darts and leaving a 6" (15 cm) opening in the seam at the bottom. Do not turn right-side out.

9 Place the shell inside the completed lining with right sides together and side seams aligned. Pin the top edges together within the seam allowance, then sew. Turn right-side out by pulling the shell through the opening in the lining seam. Handstitch the opening closed with a slip stitch. Insert the lining into the shell and finger-press the seam. Topstitch close to the edge, around the top of the bag, then again ¼" (6 mm) from the first stitch line.

Finish Tote

10 To make the handle, center the interfacing handle strip on the wrong side of the Main handle strip. Fold in half lengthwise, interfaced surfaces together, and edgestitch around the entire handle. Position the handle ends over the side seams on the outside of the bag, with the handle ends ¾" (2 cm) below the bag's top edge and topstitch a square on each handle end, through all layers, to secure them to the bag. Sew a 1⅛" (29 mm) button to each handle end, over the topstitched square.

11 To make the closure strap, center the interfacing closure strap on the wrong side of the Main closure strap. Fold in half lengthwise, interfaced surfaces together, and edgestitch around the entire strap. Sew a 1⅝" (4.1 cm) long buttonhole, ⅝" (1.5 cm) from one end of the closure strap, aligning the buttonhole parallel to the closure strap's long edges.

12 Fold the tote in half to find the center front, and mark a buttonhole placement at the center front, 1¾" (4.5 cm) above the bottom of the middle ruffle. Sew one of the

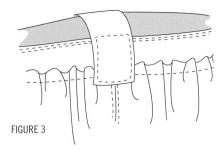

FIGURE 3

1½" (38 mm) buttons at the mark, stitching through the ruffle and the tote shell, but not the lining. Button the closure strap in place. The lower edge of the strap will fall near the bottom of the middle ruffle, while its other end extends above the bag top. Fold the strap's free end over the bag top and use basting tape to hold the strap to the bag center back, with the end of the closure strap 2½" (6.5 cm) below the bag's upper edge. Topstitch a rectangle through all layers to attach the closure strap to the bag back (**figure 3**). Sew the second 1½" (3.8 cm) button to the closure strap only, centering it 2¾" (7 cm) above the buttonhole. 🍃

CAROL ZENTGRAF is the author of *Pillows, Cushions and Tuffets; Decorative Storage; The Well-Dressed Window; Machine Embroidery Room-by-Room; Sewing for Outdoor Spaces;* and *Sewing Christmas Greetings.*

Eco Shopper
by Lisa Cox

The environmentally conscious shopper will appreciate these handy eco market bags. Sew one up in a fun print or embroider the recycling emblem on solid fabric. When not in use it folds up to fit inside a small pocket-sized pouch.

Materials

- ½ yd (46 cm) of 45" (114.5 cm) wide linen or cotton fabric (Main; for bag)
- Fat quarter (18" × 22" [45.5 × 56 cm]) of cotton print (for pouch; shown: "Save Our Planet" fabric by Fabri-Quilt Inc.)
- Embroidery floss (for optional embroidery)
- Coordinating sewing thread
- 1 package ¼" (6 mm) wide double-fold bias tape (shown: green or white)
- Fabric marking pen
- Hand-embroidery needle (for optional embroidery)
- Serger (optional)
- Small swivel hook
- Recycle Emblem embroidery template (top right) and Eco Shopper template on page 19.

Finished Size

Bag measures 15½" × 10" (39.5 × 25.5 cm). Pouch measures 4" × 6" (10 × 15 cm).

notes

* All seam allowances are ½" (1.3 cm) unless otherwise indicated.
* For explanations of terms and techniques and/or help with pattern markings, see Sewing Basics.

Cut Fabric

1 Using the pattern, cut fabric as follows:

From Main fabric:

- 2 Bag Panels on fold and transfer the dashed fold line to each of the cut pieces on the fabric wrong side.

From fat quarter:

- 1" × 2" (2.5 × 5 cm) strip
- 7" × 11" (18 × 28 cm) rectangle

Embroider Design (optional)

2 Using the Recycle Emblem embroidery template at top right, trace the emblem onto one Bag Panel using a fabric marking pen. Center the emblem from side to side, with its lowest point 5½" (14 cm) above the fabric lower edge. Using 3 strands of embroidery floss, embroider the emblem with a backstitch (see Sewing Basics, page 45).

Create Bag

3 Using a serger or the zigzag stitch on your machine and coordinating sewing thread, finish the straight edges at the top and sides of the Bag Panels. Place the front and back of the bag with right sides together and sew the seam at the top of the handle. Press the seam open, then topstitch ¼" (6 mm) from the seam line on each side.

4 Pin the bias tape over the curved edge on one side of the handle, starting and ending at the side raw edges and sliding the curved edge into the bias tape fold. Edgestitch the bias tape through all layers, making sure the back side of the tape is caught in the stitches. Repeat for the other side of the bag handle.

5 Pin the side seams of the bag right sides together and sew the side seams, catching the binding ends as well. Press the seams open and topstitch ¼" (6 mm) on each side of the seams to reinforce the sides of the bag.

6 Fold the bag along each fold line transferred from the pattern with wrong sides together and press. Fold the tote, right sides together, along each side seam and press again, forming an inverted pleat on each side of the bag. The base of the bag should measure 10" (25.5 cm).

7 Baste the lower edges together, ⅛" (3 mm) from the raw edge, to hold the pleats in place and keep the edges aligned.

8 Cut a piece of bias tape that is 12" (30.5 cm) long. Unfold the bias tape and pin it to the bag lower

Recycle Emblem

edge, right sides together and raw edges aligned; 1" (2.5 cm) of tape will extend beyond the bag at each end. Stitch the tape in place along the fold line (¼" [6 mm] from the edge). Turn the bag over. Fold both ends of the bias tape to the wrong side along the bag sides. Refold the tape along its creases, enclosing the bag raw edges, and pin in place. Edgestitch along the folded edge of the tape through all layers.

Create Pouch

9 Fold the 1" × 2" (2.5 × 5 cm) fabric strip in half lengthwise, wrong sides together, and press. Open the crease and fold the long edges to meet at the center, then press again. Refold the strip along the center crease and press, creating a ¼" × 2" (6 mm × 5 cm) strip. Edgestitch along the open edge. Fold the strip around the base of the swivel hook and baste the ends of the strip together.

10 Press ½" (1.3 cm) to the wrong side on one short end of the 7" × 11" (18 × 28 cm) rectangle. Press an additional ½" (1.3 cm) to the wrong side and edgestitch close to the first fold to hem the edge. Repeat for the other short side, so you have a rectangle measuring 7" × 9" (18 × 23 cm).

11 With the right side of the rectangle facing up, position the swivel hook on the fabric right edge, 2" (5 cm) below the top hem, and baste in place (**figure 1**).

12 Fold 3½" (9 cm) of the lower hemmed edge to the right side, forming the pouch pocket (**figure 2**). Fold 1½" (3.8 cm) of the upper hemmed edge to the right side, forming the top portion of the pouch. The pouch should now measure 4" × 7" (10 × 18 cm) with the top flap slightly overlapping the bottom flap. Sew the side seams of the pouch through all layers (**figure 3**). Serge or zigzag the raw edges of the seams together to finish. Turn the pouch right-side out, and press.

13 To fold the bag: Fold each side to meet at the bag center. Fold the bottom edge up to meet the curved handle openings and fold the handle down over the bag body. Fold about one-third of the upper portion of the bag down once more, to create a bundle small enough to slip into the fabric pouch. 🍃

LISA COX'S designs have appeared in several books, including *Pretty Little Presents* and *Sweet Nothings,* and in *Silver* magazine. Lisa blogs with her daughter, Sarah, at spoonfullofsugargirls .blogspot.com.

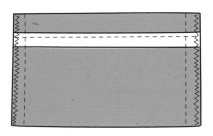
FIGURE 1

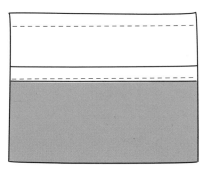
FIGURE 2

FIGURE 3

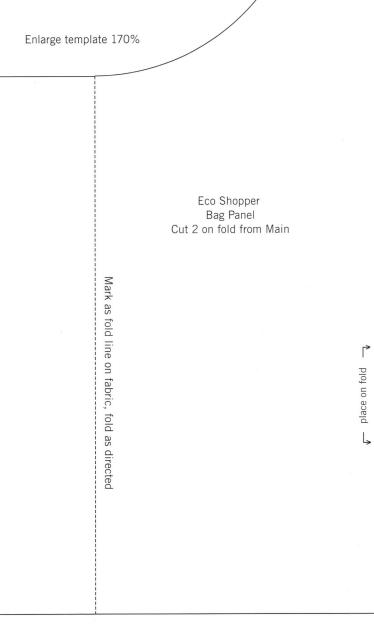

Enlarge template 170%

Eco Shopper
Bag Panel
Cut 2 on fold from Main

Mark as fold line on fabric, fold as directed

place on fold

Materials

—⅓ yd (30.5 cm) of linen (at least 56" [142 cm] wide; if using narrower fabric, use at least 42" [106.5 cm] wide fabric and see special instructions for cutting handles in Step 1)

—4 different cotton prints (each at least 42" [106.5 cm] wide, except D):

  A: ¼ yd (23 cm) of cotton print for wide stripe

  B: ½ yd (46 cm) of cotton print for thin stripe and lining

  C: ⅜ yd (34.5 cm) of cotton print for interior pocket

  D: ⅛ yd (11.5 cm) of cotton print (at least 56" [142 cm] wide; if using narrower fabric, use at least 42" [106.5 cm] wide fabric and see special instructions for cutting handles in Step 1) for thin stripe and handles

—½ yd (46 cm) of fusible fleece

—⅞ yd (80 cm) of fusible interfacing

—Matching sewing thread

—8 extra-large size (⁷⁄₁₆" [1.1 cm]) eyelets

—Setter and anvil (You can usually purchase these as a set with your grommets/eyelets.)

—Handsewing needle

—Hammer

—Acrylic ruler

—Rotary cutter and self-healing mat

—Templates on page 22

—X-Acto knife (optional)

Finished Size

15" (38 cm) long (without handles) × 18" (45.5 cm) wide. With handles, bag is about 20½" (52 cm) long.

----

note

∗ All seam allowances are ½" (1.3 cm) unless otherwise indicated.

Spring Tote

by Rashida Coleman-Hale

Combine cotton and linen for a bag that is sturdy yet stylish. The clever handle is woven through large grommets to cinch the top, and a spacious interior with large pocket provides storage for on-the-go essentials.

Cut Fabric

1 Using the templates on page 22, cut fabric as follows:

From linen:

—Cut 2 Bottom Panel on fold

—Cut 1 rectangle measuring 2 × 56" (5 × 142 cm) for handles; if your fabric is not at least 56" (142 cm)

wide, cut 2 rectangles instead, each measuring 2 × 28½" (5 × 72.5 cm) and then seam them together along one short side, using a ½" (1.3 cm) seam allowance to create one long strip measuring 56" (142 cm) long.

From cotton print A:

—Cut 2 rectangles, each measuring 6½ × 19" (16.5 × 48.5 cm) for wide stripe

From cotton print B:

—Cut 2 rectangles, each measuring 2½ × 19" (6.5 × 48.5 cm) for thin stripe

—Cut 2 Lining on fold

From cotton print C:

—Cut 1 rectangle measuring 13½ × 9" (34.5 × 23 cm) for pocket

From cotton print D:

—Cut 2 rectangles, each measuring 2½ × 19" (6.5 × 48.5 cm) for thin stripe

—Cut 1 rectangle measuring 2" × 56" (5 × 142 cm) for handles; if your fabric is not at least 56" (142 cm) wide, cut 2 rectangles instead, each measuring 2" × 28 ½" (5 × 72.5 cm) and then seam them together along one short side, using a ½" (1.3 cm) seam allowance to create one long strip measuring 56" (142 cm) long.

From fusible fleece:

—Cut 2 lining on fold, trim ½" (1.3 cm) from all edges.

From fusible interfacing:

—Cut 1 rectangle measuring 6 × 8½" (15 × 21.5 cm) for the pocket

—Cut 2 rectangles, each measuring 1¼ × 27½" (3.2 × 70 cm) for the handles

Create Shell

2 Place one of the thin stripe D pieces on top of one of the thin stripe B pieces with right sides together, lining up all edges. Pin them together along one of the long (19" [48.5 cm]) sides. Stitch them together along the pinned edge, removing pins as you go. Trim the seam allowances to ¼" (6 mm). Repeat the entire step to attach the remaining thin stripe D and B pieces.

3 Place one of the units you just created in Step 2 on top of one of the wide stripes (A) with right sides together, lining up the edge of thin stripe D with one long edge of the wide

stripe. Pin together along this edge and then stitch together, removing pins as you go. Trim seam allowances to ¼" (6 mm). Press all seam allowances up toward the wide stripe. Repeat the entire step to attach the remaining wide stripe to the other thin stripe unit created in Step 2.

4 Place one of the stripe panels you just created on one of the linen Bottom Panels with right sides together, lining up the 19" (48.5 cm) edge of the bottom stripe (B) with the top edge of the Bottom Panel. Pin and then stitch together along this edge, removing pins as you go. Trim seam allowances to ¼" (6 mm) and press up toward the stripe panel. Repeat the entire step to attach the remaining stripe panel to the remaining Bottom Panel. You now have two outer panels.

5 Lay the two completed outer panels right sides down and lay the fusible fleece pieces on top, fusible side down and centered so that the ½" (1.3 cm) seam allowances are left free. Fuse the fleece to the panels according to the manufacturer's instructions.

6 Once the fleece has been fused to the two outer panels you can quilt them if you choose to. I topstitched on the bottom of each stripe, about ⅛" (3 mm) from the seam.

7 Place the two outer panels right sides together, lining up all edges and pin around the bottom and sides. Stitch the panels together, removing pins as you go. Clip the curves of the seam allowances by cutting small triangles into the seam allowances with the points of the triangles facing the seams. Cut close to the seam, but be careful not to cut through it. Set the completed shell aside.

Create Pocket and Lining

8 Center the pocket interfacing piece on the wrong side of the top half of the pocket (C) so that the ¼" (6 mm) seam allowances are left free and fuse according to the manufacturer's instructions. Fold each edge of the pocket over to the wrong side ¼" (6 mm), folding the fabric over the interfacing, and press. Fold the pocket in half widthwise so that you have a piece measuring 6¼ × 8½" (16 × 21.5 cm) and press the fold. Topstitch through both layers along

the top 8½" (21.5 cm) edge where the two layers come together, ⅛" (3 mm) from the edge.

9 Lay one of the lining pieces (B) in front of you right-side up. Place the pocket on the lining, interfaced side down, centered left to right and 3–4" (7.5–10 cm) from the top edge of the lining. Pin in place.

10 Topstitch the pocket to the lining ⅛" (3 mm) from the side and bottom edges, making sure the pressed edges remain in place. Starting with a backstitch at one side of the pocket, stitch down to the corner and turn without lifting the needle to stitch along the bottom, then turn again at the corner to stitch up the other side and backstitch (see Sewing Basics). Leave the top of the pocket open.

11 Lay the remaining lining piece on top of the lining with the pocket, right sides together. Pin together along the sides and bottom, then stitch together, removing pins as you go. Clip the curves as in Step 7.

Assemble Bag

12 Turn the completed shell inside out and turn the shell right-side out, pull the lining up around the shell so that right sides are together and line up the top edges and side seams. Pin together around the top edge and stitch together but be sure to leave an opening in the seam that is wide enough for turning.

13 Turn the bag right-side out through the opening and then fold in the seam allowances of the opening. Press the entire bag, especially around the top so that the seams lie flat and look neat.

14 With handsewing needle and thread, stitch the opening

closed using a blindstitch (see Sewing Basics). Topstitch around the top of the bag ⅛" (3 mm) from the edge.

Add Grommets

15 With a pencil mark the spot for your first grommet about 2" (5 cm) down from the top and 2" (5 cm) over from the side seam of your bag. Make the next mark about 3" (7.5 cm) over from the first mark. Repeat these marks at the other three side seams using the same measurements.

16 Center the "male" side of one of the grommets on one of the marks and trace the inside of the grommet with a pencil. Repeat to trace the inside of the grommet around each of the marks. Using sharp scissors or an X-acto knife, cut through all layers of the bag at each drawn circle to make holes for the grommets.

17 Place the "male" end of your grommet through the hole from the wrong side (inside) of the

bag and place the anvil underneath it. Fit the "female" end of the grommet into the "male" end from the right side of the bag.

18 Be sure to do this step on a very hard, sturdy surface, such as the ground. Do not do this on any surface that you do not want to damage and be very careful of your fingers! (If you have a kit, refer to the manufacturer's instructions when attaching the grommets.)

19 Place the setter on top of the "female" end of the grommet and hammer it several times until the grommet is nice and secure. Don't over-hammer because it will cause the grommet to split. Repeat these steps with the remaining grommets.

Assemble Handles

20 Place the interfacing pieces for the handles on the wrong side of the cotton handle piece (D), placed so that ½" (1.3 cm) of the cotton fabric is left free on one long side and ¼" (6 mm) is left free on the other long side. Place the two interfacing pieces end to end, creating one long

piece of interfacing. Fuse according to manufacturer's instructions.

21 Place the cotton handle piece (D) right sides together with the linen handle piece, lining up all edges and pin together. Stitch together along the long edge with ½" (1.3 cm) seam allowance free of interfacing. Trim the seam allowances to ¼" (6 mm). Fold the linen strip over so that the strips now lie with wrong sides together. Fold the raw edges of the open side in ¼" (6 mm), press, and pin. Topstitch along this edge ⅛" (3 mm) from the edge, then topstitch ⅛" (3 mm) from the opposite edge so that you have topstitching down both long sides.

22 Lace the handle through the grommets so that the excess lengths become the handles in the center (the excess handles should lie to the outside of the bag between the two center grommets on each side). See detail photo on page 21.

23 At one raw edge of the handle, fold the raw edges in about ½" (1.3 cm) and press. Slip the other raw edge of the handle inside the folded edge about ½" (1.3 cm) so that the side seams of the handle match up and the handle lies flat. Topstitch through all layers ⅛" (3 mm) from the folded edge. Backstitch a few times to make sure it's secure. Slide the handle along so that the seam is hidden on the inside of the bag, and you're done! 🍃

RASHIDA COLEMAN-HALE is the author of *I Love Patchwork*.

Lining
Cut 2 on fold

place on fold

Enlarge both templates 300%

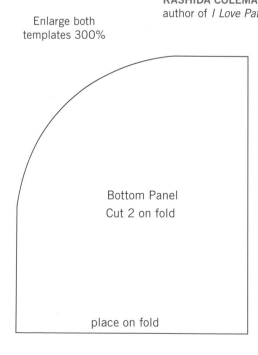

Bottom Panel
Cut 2 on fold

place on fold

Fabulous Tote Bag
by Kathy York

This fabulous little tote bag is perfect for carrying all your essentials. It is just the right size to be big enough, yet not so big that you are tempted to put too many items in it, thus weighing you down all day and putting a crick in your back. It is lined with a bright fabric so that when you look inside, you can find what you are looking for. The strap is quilted, which makes it oh-so-comfortable to carry. And if it gets dirty, it is 100-percent machine washable. It is easy to make and just small enough to practice your machine quilting skills without the hard work of pushing an entire quilt under your machine.

Materials

—Fabric for lower portion of bag, 2 rectangles each 5" × 14" (12.5 × 35.5 cm)

—Fabric for upper portion of bag, 2 rectangles each 10" × 14" (25.5 × 35.5 cm)

—Fabric for lining, 2 squares each 14" × 14" (35.5 × 35.5 cm)

—Fabric for interior pocket, 6" × 9" (15 × 23 cm) rectangle

—Fabric for strap, 38" × 4" (96.5 × 10 cm) strip

—Muslin, 2 rectangles each 15" × 15" (38 × 38 cm)

—Prewashed batting, 2 rectangles each 15" × 15" (38 × 38 cm), 1 strip 38" × 2" (96.5 × 5 cm)

—Scissors

—Matching thread

—Clear, gridded ruler such as Omnigrid

—Fabric marking pencil

—Iron and ironing surface

—Sewing machine

—Optional

—Scotchguard

---

note

* Sew seams with fabric right sides together, using a ½" (1.3 cm) seam allowance unless otherwise indicated.

Front and Back

1 For the bag front, sew the long edges of one upper and one lower rectangle together. Repeat for the bag back. You should have two pieced squares, each measuring 14" × 14" (35.5 × 35.5 cm).

2 Make 2 quilt sandwiches by centering each pieced square right-side up on a square of batting and then muslin. Pin, then machine quilt the layers together. Trim the quilted squares to 14" × 14" (35.5 × 35.5 cm).

3 With right sides together, sew the quilted squares together along the side and bottom edges, leaving the top open. Do not turn right-side out.

4 To create the bottom of the bag, line up the seam of 1 side with the bottom seam and pin together. This will bring the bottom corners into a

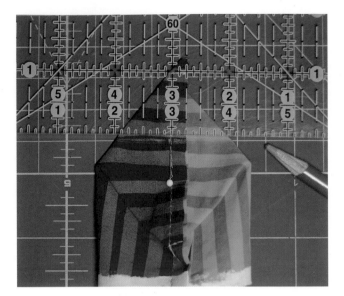

FIGURE 1 *Note:* The sample in the photo is not the same scale as the tote bag.

point of a diamond shape with the seam coming straight up the middle (**figure 1**). Position a clear, gridded ruler on top of the seam as shown, and move the ruler up or down along the seam until the distance across the triangle is 2½" (6.5 cm), keeping the ruler aligned with the seam. Use a pencil to mark this line, and then stitch along it. Repeat for the other corner.

Lining and Pocket

5 Fold the pocket rectangle in half, right sides together, creating a 4½" × 6" (11.5 × 15 cm) rectangle. Sew the side seams.

6 Turn the pocket right-side out. Turn the raw edges ½" (1.3 cm) to the inside and press. Sew a narrow edgestitch across the folded edge, sewing through all layers. This folded/stitched edge will be the top edge of the pocket.

7 Pin the pocket to the right side of 1 lining square, placing it 2½" (6.5 cm) from the top edge and centering it between the side edges. Topstitch the pocket in place, stitching ⅛" (3 mm) from the pocket edges (leave the top open to create the pocket).

8 With right sides together, sew the lining squares together, leaving the top edge open and leaving a 5" (12.5 cm) opening along the bottom edge. Repeat Step 4 to create the boxed bottom corners. Do not turn the lining right-side out.

Strap

9 Fold the strip of strap fabric in half lengthwise, right sides together. Pin the batting on top. Sew ¼" (6 mm) seams along both long edges. Turn the tube right-side out and press.

10 Machine quilt a fun design along the length of the strap.

Finish

11 Turn the tote bag right-side out.

12 Pin the strap ends to the top edge of the tote at both side seams, making sure the strap is not twisted and the raw edges are aligned. (The strap should go down the sides and around the bottom edge of the tote bag.) Sew the straps in place, using a ¼" (6 mm) seam allowance. This is a reinforcing seam, allowing you to remove the pins.

13 Place the tote bag inside the lining with right sides together, side seams aligned, and top edges even. (The strap will be hidden inside.) Sew the tote and lining together, stitching ½" (1.3 cm) from the top edge. Turn the bag right-side out by pulling the tote and straps through the opening in the lining.

14 Press under the seam allowances on the opening and edgestitch the opening closed. Push the lining to the inside of the tote bag.

15 Topstitch along the top edge of the tote/lining, and along the straps. If desired, spray the outside of the bag with Scotchguard so it will stay clean longer. 🍃

Visit **KATHY YORK'S** blog at aquamoonartquilts.blogspot.com.

Materials
For 1 tote bag and 2 interchangeable pockets

—Cotton canvas or duck cloth in a neutral shade for the tote bag body, 1 yd (91.5 cm)

—Assorted cotton prints for the patchwork pocket fronts, 2 yd (183 cm) total

—Muslin for the patchwork pocket lining, ½ yd (46 cm)

—¾" (2 cm) wide Velcro Fabric Fusion tape, 6 yd (5.5 m)

—Accent button, 2 (1 per pocket)

—Elastic cord, 6" (15 cm) length

—Pocket template on page 26

—Parchment paper

Finished Size
14¼" × 15" (36 × 38 cm; tote bag body), 14¼" × 12" (36 × 30.5 cm; pocket)

---

note

✳ Use ¼" (6 mm) seam allowances unless otherwise noted.

Directions

1 From the canvas, cut 2 rectangles 16½" × 18¼" (42 × 46.5 cm). Layer the rectangles, wrong sides together, and sew around 3 sides, leaving 1 of the narrow sides open, this will be the top of the bag.

2 Clip the 2 bottom corners of the bag, turn it inside out, and press. Stitch again around the 3 sides, this time using a ½" (1.3 cm) seam allowance, hiding the seam from Step 1 (**figure 1**). Then turn the bag body again so it is right-side out.

3 For the bag straps, cut 2 strips of canvas 3" × 27" (7.5 × 68.5 cm). Turn ¼" (6 mm) to the wrong side on the long edges, fold down the middle, and topstitch ⅛" (3 mm) from the edge along both long sides. Do the same for both straps.

Note: You can also use 1¼" (3.2 cm) wide cotton webbing for the straps. Simply cut (2) 27" (68.5 cm) lengths and proceed.

4 Turn the top raw edge of the bag body 1" (2.5 cm) to the wrong side and press. Repeat.

A Personalized Tote
WITH INTERCHANGEABLE POCKETS

by J. Ana Flores Beckett

This tote has a switchable patchwork pocket, making it a fun accessory to customize according to seasons, your outfit, or your mood. The pocket is attached to the tote with Velcro strips along the sides and bottom. An accent button and an elastic loop at the top of the pocket help to keep it in place. You can create as many pockets for one tote as you wish; the instructions are for two pockets. This is a great dual-purpose project that both beginning and advanced sewers will enjoy.

5 Attach the bag straps from Step 3 to the bag body by slipping the strap ends under the turned-down strip of fabric on the top, centering, and pinning (figure 2). Sew along the bottom of the turned strip, as well as the top, securing the straps and the top hem with these seams.

6 Using the assorted print fabrics, piece a patchwork panel from which to cut the first pocket. (I used a ½" (1.3 cm) seam allowance to join strips together in wonky lines, pressing seams toward darker fabrics.) Trace the pocket template onto a piece of parchment paper, cut it out, and use it as a gauge to make sure the pieced panel will accommodate the size and shape of the pocket (figure 3).

> **Tip**
>
> Parchment paper is wonderful to use as a template. When you place it on top of the patchwork, you can see through it and determine where you want to make your cuts.

7 You will cut the muslin lining and the pocket patchwork in one step. Layer the muslin on the bottom and place the patchwork panel on top (right-side up). Position the parchment paper template as desired on the patchwork panel and pin in place, pinning through all layers. Cut out the pocket shape, cutting through all the layers.

8 With right sides together, sew the muslin piece to the pocket using a ½" (1.3 cm) seam allowance and leaving 3" (7.5 cm) open for turning. Clip the corners, turn the pocket right-side out, press, and blindstitch the opening closed.

9 Stitch the patchwork pieces in the ditch to secure them to the muslin lining.

> **Tip**
>
> Personalize the pocket by creating a different patchwork pattern, or try using different free-motion stitching patterns.

10 Repeat Steps 6–9 for the second patchwork pocket.

11 Cut 3 lengths of the fusible Velcro measuring (a) 11¾" (30 cm), (b) 13½" (34.5 cm), and (c) 8¼" (21 cm). Curve the tops of (a) and (c) to accommodate the slopes on the pocket.

12 Following the manufacturer's instructions, fuse the strips to the tote bag body, with (a) along the left side and flush with the bottom edge, (b) flush along the bottom, and (c) along the right side, flush with the top edge of (b) (figure 4).

13 Fuse the opposite side of the Velcro strips to the muslin side of the pocket. Sew an accent button to the top center of the pocket, and sew a corresponding loop of elastic to the tote.

14 Repeat Step 13 for the second patchwork pocket, using a second button to match up with the loop already sewn to the tote. Switch out the pockets as you wish, and enjoy! 🍃

J. ANA FLORES BECKETT blogs at thegirlwithacurl.com.

FIGURE 1

FIGURE 2

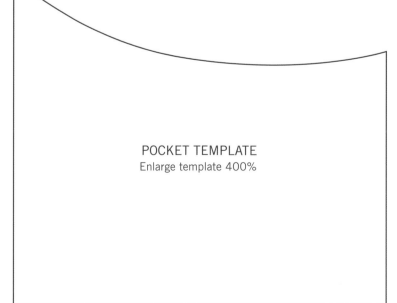

FIGURE 3

FIGURE 4

POCKET TEMPLATE
Enlarge template 400%

Materials
For 1 convertible tote.

—Feature fabric (quilting weight), ½ yd (46 cm)

—Contrast lining fabric (quilting weight), ½ yd (46 cm)

—Accent fabric for the shoulder strap, handles, and interior pocket (quilting weight), ½ yd (46 cm)

—Mid-weight woven, fusible interfacing, 1 yd (91.5 cm)

—20" (51 cm) wide fusible fleece, ⅔ yd (60 cm; I use Pellon Thermolam.)

—Fusible web, ¼ yd (23 cm)

—Heavy variegated quilting thread that contrasts against your fabric (I use YLI fusions.)

—Piecing thread in a solid neutral color

—Ribbon or twill tape for the key leash, 18" (45.5 cm)

—1" (2.5 cm) metal tri-glide strap adjuster, 1

—1" (2.5 cm) D-rings, 2

—1" (2.5 cm) swivel snap clips, 2

—Rotary cutting supplies

—Sewing machine with a walking foot and a free motion foot

—Bird templates on page 29

Finished Size
12" wide × 14" tall (30.5 × 35.5 cm)

---

notes

SEAMS: All seams are ½" (1.3 cm).

TOPSTITCH: Using a strong, sharp needle, thick thread, and a slightly longer stitch length, stitch very close to the edge of the seam. You may want to repeat this with a second line of stitching about ⅜" (1 cm) in from the outer edge as well.

BASTE: Sew with a long stitch length ¼" (6 mm) in from the raw edge.

Cut the Fabrics and Prepare the Lining

1 Cut out all fabric pieces according to the Cutting Chart on page 28.

2 Center and fuse the interfacing to the wrong side of the bag lining. (If you are using a fabric that's on the heavier end of quilting-weight fabrics (such as a Kona cotton) you can eliminate this step.

Convertible Tote
THREE BAGS IN ONE
by Candy Glendening

This tote is actually three different bags in one. The shoulder strap is attached several inches from the top, so the top of the bag can either fold over to close, or be folded open for easy access. The bag interior features a divided slip pocket and a key leash, to help keep smaller items organized and accessible. The busy patterns found in Daisy Janie's "Shades of Grey" fabric line are balanced with bright jewel-tone hand-dyed fabrics, and the cute fused bird appliqués add just the right amount of quirky character.

Prepare the Outside of the Bag

3 Center the fusible fleece on the outside main and bottom pieces, with the rough side of the fleece facing the wrong side of the fabric. Fuse the fleece to the fabric by firmly pressing with steam on the right side of the fabric.

Note: Do not touch the fleece directly with a hot iron; it will melt onto your iron.

4 Use a walking foot to quilt the 2 main bag pieces (the featured bags were quilted with a gray thread in uneven lines that roughly parallel the designs in the fabric).

5 Select several of the bird patterns (for use on the front and back main pieces) and trace them onto the paper side of the fusible web; cut out roughly, cutting just beyond the drawn lines. Following the manufacturer's directions, iron the fusible web birds to the wrong side of scraps of the lining and accent fabrics. Cut out the birds, remove the paper, and arrange the birds on the bottom third of the main outside pieces, keeping the ½" (1.3 cm) seam allowance in mind.

Note: The main pieces are only slightly taller than they are wide. Make sure you place the birds so they're walking along the bottom of the bag, not up the side!

6 When the placement of the birds has been determined fuse only the top of each bird. Then "free-motion machine sketch" (FMMS) the legs, beginning and ending underneath the bottom of each bird (**figure 1a**). Then fuse the rest of the bird over the tops of the legs and FMMS an outline for each bird (**figure 1b**). Finish by fusing and FMMSing the bird wings and adding a stitched eye (**figure 1c**).

7 With right sides together, stitch the contrasting bottom fabric to the bottom of the outside main pieces. Press these seams open, being careful not to touch the fleece with your iron. Topstitch along each side of the seam.

Process photos by Candy Glendening

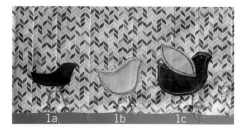

FIGURES 1A, 1B, AND 1C

Prepare the Pocket and the Straps

8 Fold the pocket fabric in half (so that it is 13" wide × 5½" tall [33 × 14 cm]) and press. Open the fabric and place the fusible batting along the crease (center the batting width-wise). Refold the fabric and press with a hot steam iron. Topstitch along the top folded edge.

9 If you only have the minimum fabric required you will have to piece the 4" × 60" (10 × 152.5 cm) strap

CUTTING CHART

# to cut from:			fabric	interfacing	fusible fleece
Fabric	Piece		h × w	h × w	h × w
Feature	Outside Main	2	13½" × 13" (34.5 × 33 cm)	-	12½" × 12" (31.5 × 30.5 cm)
Lining	Outside Bottom	2	2½" × 13" (6.5 × 33 cm)	-	1½" × 12" (3.8 × 30.5 cm)
Lining	Lining	2	15" × 13" (38 × 33 cm)	14¾" × 12¾" (37.5 × 32 cm)	-
Accent	Handle	2	9" × 4" (23 × 10 cm)	9" × 2" (23 × 5 cm)	-
Accent	Divided Pocket	1	11" × 13" (28 × 33 cm)	-	5" × 12" (12.5 × 30.5 cm)
Accent	Strap*	1	60" × 4" (152.5 × 10 cm)	60" × 2" (152.5 × 5 cm)	-
Accent	D-ring Loops	2	2" × 4" (5 × 10 cm)	2" × 2" (5 × 5 cm)	-

*For the strap, piece 4" (10 cm) × WOF (width of fabric) strips end-to end to make a 60" (152.5 cm) long strip. It is not necessary to piece the interfacing strips for the handle, just cut enough interfacing strips to add up to 60" (152.5 cm).

> ### Free-Motion Machine Sketching
>
> What I call "Free-Motion Machine Sketching" is very similar to free-motion machine quilting: feed dogs down, darning foot, needle going quickly, and hands moving slowly. The difference is that when I'm sketching, I am purposefully retracing my steps and intentionally trying to miss. This took some practice after years of trying to follow lines exactly. What I'm trying to emphasize here is that although I'm using a machine, the process is still created by my hands! I love the beautiful imperfection of a strong line that is created by drawing it over and over—it's just that my pencil is an electric sewing machine.

Convertible Tote
bird templates

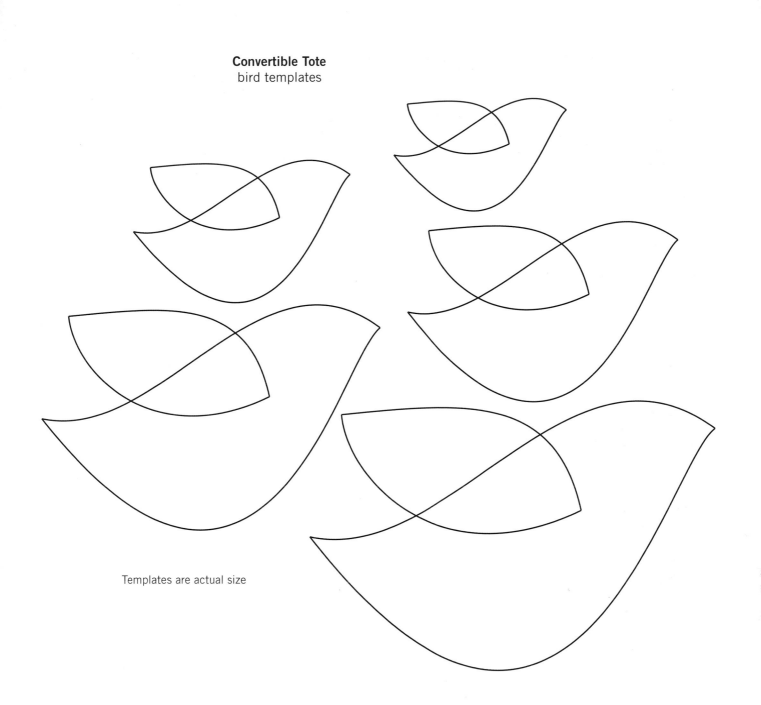

Templates are actual size

(press the seam open). Center and fuse the interfacing to the wrong side of the strap, handles, and D-ring loops. Fold and press the sides of all these units so that they meet in the center. Then fold in half lengthwise and press so they are 1" (2.5 cm) wide with all raw edges enclosed. Topstitch along both of the folded edges for all pieces.

10 Attach the long strap to the center of the tri-glide by passing it around the center, folding the raw end under, and stitching that end to the strap. Reinforce it by stitching back and forth a few times. Thread the free end of the strap through 1 of the swivel snaps and then up and down through each side of the tri-glide and then finally through the second swivel snap. Fold the raw end under and stitch it to the strap. Reinforce it by stitching back and forth a few times.

Tip

You can make the pockets any size you want. Simply pin the outside edges of the pocket to the lining, place your desired items in this large mock pocket and pin where appropriate. Remove the items; mark the location of the seams, remove the marking pins, and stitch.

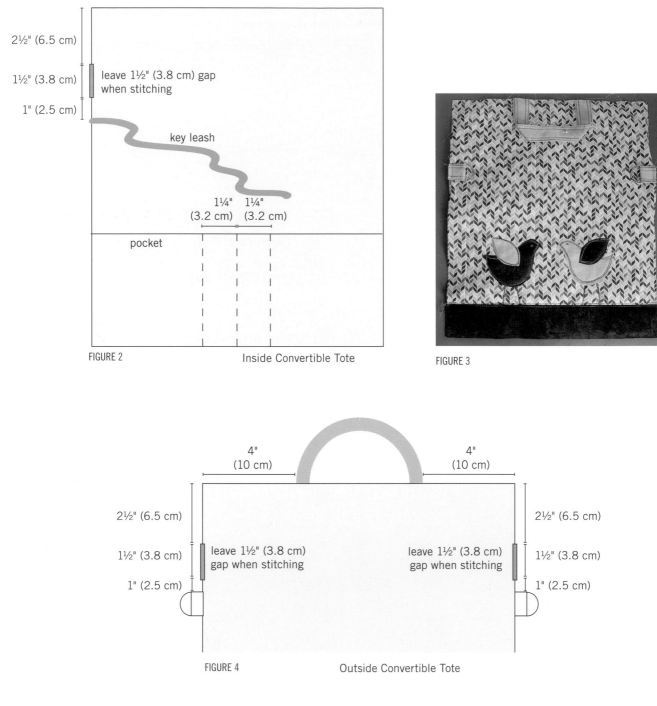

2½" (6.5 cm)

1½" (3.8 cm) — leave 1½" (3.8 cm) gap when stitching

1" (2.5 cm)

key leash

1¼" (3.2 cm) 1¼" (3.2 cm)

pocket

FIGURE 2   Inside Convertible Tote

FIGURE 3

4" (10 cm)   4" (10 cm)

2½" (6.5 cm)   2½" (6.5 cm)

1½" (3.8 cm) — leave 1½" (3.8 cm) gap when stitching   leave 1½" (3.8 cm) gap when stitching — 1½" (3.8 cm)

1" (2.5 cm)   1" (2.5 cm)

FIGURE 4   Outside Convertible Tote

Assemble the Bag

11 Align the raw edges of the pocket with the sides and the bottom of 1 of the lining pieces and pin. Attach the pocket to the lining by stitching up the center. Backstitch at the top edge of the seam to reinforce it. Stitching another seam 1¼" (3.2 cm) on either side of the center will create 2 pen slips and 2 cell phone–sized pockets (**figure 2**).

12 Baste the ribbon along a side of the lining 5" (12.5 cm) down from the top. Pin the other edge of the ribbon in the center of the lining so you don't accidentally stitch it while assembling the bag. On the wrong side of the lining, mark a 1½" (3.8 cm) gap that is 2½" (6.5 cm) down from the top on both sides (**figure 2**). (In the finished bag, these gaps will allow for the D-rings to slip through the layers when the top of the bag is folded down as shown in **figure 7**.)

13 Baste the tote handles on the top of each outer bag piece 4" (10 cm) in from each side. Wrap the D-ring loops around the D-rings and baste them 4½" (11.5 m) down from the top on the sides of 1 of the outer bag pieces (**figure 3**).

14 On the wrong side of the outer bag piece, mark a 1½" (3.8 cm) gap that is 2½" (6.5 cm) down from the top on both sides (**figure 4**).

15 Pin the 2 lining pieces with the right sides together. Stitch down 1 side, across the bottom and up the other side, leaving the marked gaps open and backstitching at the top and bottom of each gap (**figure 5**). Press the seams open. Repeat this with the outside bag pieces.

16 Topstitch around the 4 gaps in the side seams (**figure 6**). Trim the bottom corners of both the bag and the lining to reduce bulk. Turn the lining right-side out, and place the lining inside the bag with the right sides together. Align the side

seams, and pin the raw edges of the top of the lining and bag together.

17 Stitch around the top, leaving a gap large enough for your hand, and backstitching where the handles are attached to reinforce them. Turn the bag right-side out through the gap. Press the top well and topstitch all the way around, making sure to stitch the gap closed.

18 Attach the strap to the D-rings. Note that when you wish to have the tote top folded open, the D-rings will slip through the gaps in the side seams (**figure 7**). 🖉

Visit **CANDY GLENDENING'S** website at candiedfabrics.com.

Tip

You can make the pockets any size you want. Simply pin the outside edges of the pocket to the lining, place your desired items in this large mock pocket, and pin where appropriate. Remove the items; mark the location of the seams, remove the marking pins, and stitch.

FIGURE 5

FIGURE 6

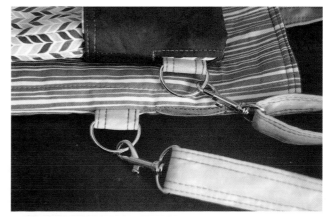

FIGURE 7

Materials

- 1¼ yd (1.4 m) of 45–54" (114.5–137 cm) wide 100% cotton home decorator fabric (denim or duck cloth would also work)
- 1¾ yd (1.6 m) of 20" (51 cm) wide heavyweight nonwoven (sew-in or fusible) interfacing
- Multicolor machine quilting and all-purpose sewing thread
- Two 1⅛" (28 mm) round wooden buttons
- Rotary cutter and self-healing mat (optional)
- Point turner or similar tool (such as a chopstick)
- Removable fabric marking tool
- Drinking glass or similar round object or a French curve (for rounding corners)
- Handsewing needle

Finished Size

13" long (without handle) × 15" wide (33 × 38 cm). With handle, tote is 22½" (57 cm) long.

notes

- All seam allowances are ½" (1.3 cm) unless otherwise noted.
- For explanations of terms and techniques, see Sewing Basics.
- All topstitching was sewn with multicolor machine quilting thread.
- Buttons were sewn on with multicolor machine quilting thread.

Cut the Fabric

1 Cut the following pieces as directed from the home decorator fabric:

- Four 16" × 13½" (40.5 × 34.5 cm) pieces for bag and bag lining
- One 40" × 5" (101.5 × 12.5 cm) piece for gusset
- Two 20½" × 5" (52 × 12.5 cm) pieces for gusset lining
- Four 8" × 3" (20.5 × 7.5 cm)-wide pieces for tabs
- One 26" × 4" (66 × 10 cm) piece for handle

2 Cut the following pieces as directed from the heavyweight nonwoven interfacing:

Arrow Tab Tote

by June McCrary Jacobs

Stitch up your own roomy tote using durable, washable 100% cotton home décor fabric. The unique sideways strap combined with the arrow tabs and wooden buttons make this an eye-catching way to transport your must-have stuff.

—Two 16" × 13½" (40.5 × 34.5 cm) pieces for bag

—One 40" × 5" (101.5 × 12.5 cm) piece for gusset

—Two 8" × 3" (20.5 × 7.5 cm) pieces for tabs

—One 26" × 4" (66 × 10 cm) piece for handle

Sew the Tabs

3 Baste the interfacing to the wrong side of two tab rectangles; if the interfacing is fusible, follow the manufacturer's instructions to fuse it in place. Measure and mark both long edges of each rectangle 1" (2.5 cm) from one short end and mark the center of the same short end. Draw a line connecting the marks to indicate a pointed end for the tab (**figure 1**). Pair each interfaced rectangle with one of the remaining tab rectangles, right sides together, and pin. Cut along the marked lines to form the pointed end.

4 Sew each tab along the long edges and the short pointed end, using a ¼" (6 mm) seam allowance, leaving the short straight edge open for turning. Trim the corners and turn the tabs right-side out. Use a point turner or other tool to gently work the corners into place, then press flat. Topstitch around each tab, ⅜" (1 cm) from the finished edges.

5 With a removable marking tool, measure and mark the centerline of each tab, beginning at the point. Measure and mark perpendicular to the centerline 1" (2.5 cm) above the point. Use this placement guide to work a 1¼" (3.2 cm) long buttonhole along the centerline of each tab, beginning 1" (2.5 cm) above the point. *Note:* If using a different size button, recalculate the buttonhole length. Set tabs aside.

Sew the Handle

6 Press the handle in half lengthwise, wrong sides together. Open the fold and position the interfacing on the fabric wrong side, with one long edge along the crease and extending to the left. If using fusible interfacing, press to fuse. Fold both long edges of the handle fabric to the wrong side to meet at the center crease, enclosing the interfacing, and press.

7 Refold the handle fabric along the original crease and press once more, enclosing the fabric edges.

8 Topstitch the handle long edges ¼" (6 mm) and ⅜" (1 cm) from the edges. Set handle aside.

Sew the Bag

9 Baste or fuse interfacing to the wrong sides of two 16" × 13½" (40.5 × 34.5 cm) bag rectangles.

10 Lay one interfaced rectangle crosswise on a flat work surface. Using a drinking glass or French curve as a guide, round the two lower corners, tracing the curve with a removable marking pen. If the fabric is a directional print, make sure the print runs correctly from top to bottom. Trim the fabric along the curved guidelines, rounding the corners.

11 Repeat Step 10 for the bag back, using the first rectangle as a guide to ensure the curved corners are consistent. Repeat Step 10 again with the remaining fabric bag pieces; these are the lining and are not interfaced.

12 Baste or fuse the gusset interfacing to the gusset.

13 Pin the interfaced gusset to one of the interfaced bag pieces, right sides together, pinning from one square upper corner, around the bottom, and to the other square corner. Stitch; press the seam allowances toward the bag piece.

14 Topstitch around the bag piece, ⅜" (1 cm) from the gusset seam, catching the seam allowances in the stitching.

15 Repeat Steps 13–14 to attach the remaining interfaced bag piece to the other side of the gusset.

16 Sew the two fabric gusset lining pieces together at one short edge. Press the seam allowances open.

17 Assemble the bag lining as in Steps 13 and 15, omitting the topstitching in Step 14, using the gusset lining piece and the remaining bag pieces (without interfacing). Leave an 8" (20.5 cm) gap in one seam along the bottom edge of the tote for turning. Set the lining aside.

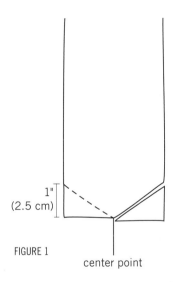

1" (2.5 cm)

FIGURE 1

center point

18 Determine which side of the bag will be the back. Measure and mark the tote back's upper edge 2¼" (5.5 cm) from each side seam. Position the assembled tabs on the tote back, right sides together, with the outer edge of the tab along the mark. The tab raw edge should extend ½" (1.3 cm) beyond the bag raw edge. Stitch ¼" (6 mm) from the tote raw edge to baste and reinforce the tabs.

19 Fold the tote front and back to find the centers of the upper edges. Center the handle on the back, right sides together, with the handle end extending ½" (1.3 cm) beyond the bag raw edge, and pin. Bring the handle down and under the tote bottom, then center the handle's other end on the tote front, right sides together, again extending the handle end ½" (1.3 cm) beyond the bag raw edge. Make sure the handle is not twisted. Pin, then baste both handle ends ¼" (6 mm) from the tote raw edge.

20 With the bag right-side out and the bag lining wrong-side out, slip the bag into the lining, right sides together, matching the upper edges. Sew the bag and lining together along the upper edge, catching the tab and handle ends in the seam.

21 Reach through the gap in the lining seam and turn the tote right-side out. Tuck the lining into the tote and press the upper edge, pressing the tabs and handle away from the bag. Topstitch ⅛" (3 mm) and ⅜" (1 cm) from the upper edge.

22 Slip-stitch the gap in the lining seam closed.

23 To make a pleat in the top edge of the gusset, fold the gusset in half, lengthwise, with right sides together. Working inside the bag, sew the gusset layers together by stitching over the previous ⅜" (1 cm) topstitching from the fold to a point ¼" (6 mm) short of the bag side seam (**figure 2**). Repeat on the other side of the bag.

24 Mark buttonhole placements on the bag front 3½" (9 cm) from the side seams and 4" (10 cm) below the bag's upper edge. Sew a button to each placement mark. Fold the tabs over the top of the bag and button to close. 🍃

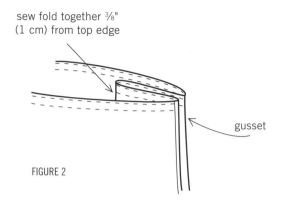

sew fold together ⅜" (1 cm) from top edge

gusset

FIGURE 2

JUNE MCCRARY JACOBS'S designs and articles have been published in several sewing and crafting magazines and books. Contact her at usajunedesigns@ yahoo.com.

Calendar Patchwork TOTE

by Susan Wasinger

Transform vintage kitchen calendar towels into an eco-friendly tote to take you to the market in style. Create the patchwork by cutting out interesting graphic words and images from the towels for a one-of-a-kind design.

Materials
—¾ yd (68.5 cm) of cotton canvas or duck

—2 or 3 (or more) cotton or linen vintage kitchen calendar towels

—Matching thread

—Handsewing needle

—Tailor's chalk or marking pen

—Acrylic quilt ruler

Finished Size
17½" (44.5) at the widest top opening tapering to 11" (28 cm) wide at the bottom × 16½" (42 cm) tall.

Cut Out Fabric

1 Cut 2 pieces of 19" × 4½" (48 × 11.5 cm) cotton canvas or duck for the top band.

2 For the 2 central patchwork bands (1 for each side of the bag), I pieced fabrics together so the finished patchwork bands measured 19" × 8½" (48 × 21.5 cm) each. See Steps 5 and 6 for instructions.

3 For the bottom of the tote bag, cut a 19" × 19" (48 × 48 cm) square of cotton canvas or duck.

4 Cut 4 pieces of fabric, each 2" × 23" (5 × 58.5 cm) for the 2 straps.

Create Patchwork Pieces

5 To create the 2 patchwork inserts, cut interesting graphics, both words and images, from the vintage kitchen linens. The pieces can be different sizes and shapes if you so desire.

6 Machine stitch the individual pieces together with ¼" (6 mm) seams, then use a zigzag stitch to finish the seam allowances. The finished pieces should each be cut to 19" × 8½" (48 × 21.5 cm). See **figure 1** for the basic shapes I chose to use for my patchwork band.

Assembly

Note: Use ⅜" (1 cm) seam allowances for this section unless otherwise indicated.

7 With right sides together, machine stitch one of the top bands onto the top edge of one of the patchwork inserts.

8 With right sides together, machine stitch the bottom edge of this same patchwork insert to the bottom body piece of the bag.

9 At the other end of this main piece, attach the other patchwork insert as in Step 8.

10 At the other end of the patchwork insert just used, attach the other top band, as in Step 7.

11 Fold this large fabric piece in half, right sides together, making sure the bands of patchwork match up along the sides. Machine stitch the side seams and finish them by zigzagging the seam allowances together.

12 Turn the bag right-side out and fold down the top edge of the bag, toward the wrong side ½" (1.3 cm), then fold over again 1" (2.5 cm). Pin and topstitch around the perimeter of the bag, about ¾"–⅞" (2–2.2 cm) in from the edge.

13 To give the bag structure, create a bottom gusset as follows: Turn the bag inside out and lay it flat in front of you so the bottom corner is pointing up and the side seam is running directly down the center. Measure in from the corner about 3¼" (8.5 cm) and mark a line across the width (from edge to edge). This line will be about 6" (15 cm) long. Machine stitch through both layers

along the line (**figure 2**). Repeat on the other side at the opposite bottom corner of the bag. It makes a stronger bottom if you leave the excess fabric in place instead of trimming the seam. When you turn the bag right-side out, you will have a flat bottom created by the seams.

Make and Attach Straps

14 Pin 2 of the strap pieces together with right sides facing. Machine stitch ¼" (6 mm) seams along the long sides and one of the short ends. Trim the corners and turn right-side out. Tuck in the raw edges on the open end and hand- or machine-stitch closed. Repeat entire step with the remaining strap pieces.

15 Mark the positions for the four places the straps will attach to the bag along the top edge (2 on each side). Each should be about 5½" (14 cm) in from the side seams.

16 Tuck the strap end about 1½" (3.8 cm) into the bag's interior and pin in place. Topstitch horizontally across the top and bottom of the 1½" (3.8 cm) of handle that is inside the bag, with the bottom stitching lying right over the topstitching already in place. Backstitch (see Sewing Basics) repeatedly to reinforce the connection. Repeat entire step

to attach the other end of the same strap to the other mark on the same side of the bag. Repeat entire step again to attach the remaining strap to the opposite side of the bag. 🍃

SUSAN WASINGER is the author of *Fabricate* and *Sewn by Hand.* Her work has also appeared in *Natural Home* and *Metropolitan Home Magazine* and she has been featured on HGTV's *Look What I Did.*

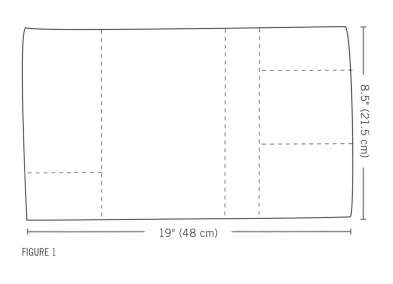

FIGURE 1

19" (48 cm)

8.5" (21.5 cm)

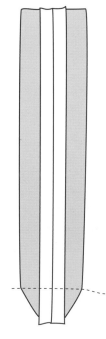

FIGURE 2

Firewood Tote
by Erin Harris

This stylish tote is the perfect solution for carrying and corralling firewood as well as adding a pretty pop of color to your hearth. The large-scale home décor print fabric panel becomes the star, featured against a solid-color background. Sturdy jute webbing straps make transporting that heavy load a snap.

Materials

—3 yd (2.7 m) of 59" (150 cm) wide cotton duck for shell and lining (Main)

—1 yd (91.5 cm) of 54" (137 cm) wide home decorator print fabric for panels (Contrast)

—4½ yd (4.1 m) of 3½" (9 cm) wide jute upholstery webbing for straps and handles

—Matching sewing thread

—Tailor's chalk

—Handsewing needle

—Template on page 39

Finished Size
26" wide × 18" high × 12" deep
(66 × 45.5 × 30.5 cm)

---

notes

---

* All seam allowances are ½" (1.3 cm) unless otherwise noted.

* For explanations of terms and techniques, see Sewing Basics.

Cut the Fabric

1 Photocopy the template piece on page 39, enlarging by 400%. From Main fabric, cut 4 Tote Body on the fold (2 for shell, 2 for lining).

2 From Contrast fabric, cut 2 panels, each 25" long × 15" wide (63.5 × 38 cm).

3 Cut two 75" (1.9 m) lengths of the jute upholstery webbing.

Make the Handles

4 Fold one 75" (1.9 m) length of webbing in half widthwise to find the center and mark it with a pin or chalk. Measure 8" (20.5 cm) in each direction from the center and mark across the entire webbing width with pins or chalk.

5 Fold the webbing in half lengthwise and pin the long edges together within the 16" (40.5 cm) span between the marks just made. Starting at one mark, sew the webbing together, ⅛" (3 mm) from the edge, until you reach the other end mark. Leave the needle in the down position, pivot 90 degrees, and sew across the folded webbing until you are ⅛" (3 mm) from the opposite (folded) edge. Pivot again in the same manner and continue sewing ⅛" (3 mm) from the folded edge, back to the first end mark. Pivot again and sew back to the beginning of your stitch line **(figure 1)**. Make a final pivot and overlap the stitches for ½" (1.3 cm), then backtack to secure.

6 Repeat Steps 4–5 for the other handle.

Assemble the Shell Pieces

7 Center a Contrast fabric panel (right-side up) on the right side of one Tote Body, matching raw edges at the top and the bottom. Pin and then sew the panel to the Tote Body by topstitching ¼" (6 mm) from each edge of the panel.

8 Pin one handle to the same Tote Body, aligning the webbing raw edges with the bottom edge of the tote; make sure the handle is not twisted and that the stitched 16"

(40.5 cm) portion of the handle is centered over the top edge of the Tote Body **(figure 2)**. The webbing's outer edge will be 6" (15 cm) from the bottom corner and 1" (2.5 cm) from the top corner on each side of the Tote Body, and the webbing will overlap the Contrast panel side edges 1½" (3.8 cm) on each side. Use chalk or pins to mark the webbing edges 2" (5 cm) below the tote upper edge. Beginning at the bottom raw edges, sew each side of the handle in place by topstitching ⅛" (3 mm) from the webbing edges, pivoting at the marks to sew across the webbing, and then pivoting again to stitch down the other side as in Step 5 **(figure 1)**. Pivot once more and continue sewing ¼" (6 mm) from the bottom raw edges to baste the webbing to the fabric.

9 Repeat Steps 7–8 with another Tote Body and the remaining Contrast panel and handle. These are the shell pieces.

Sew the Tote

10 With right sides together, pin the assembled shell pieces together along the bottom and side edges only (see pattern). Sew all three seams and then press the seams open.

11 To form the bottom of the tote, box the corners by flattening the tote to align one side seam with the bottom seam. Pin together and then sew ½" (1.3 cm) from the edge **(figure 3)**. Repeat to box the other side of the tote.

12 Repeat Steps 10–11 for the lining, leaving a 10" (25.5 cm) opening in the bottom seam.

13 Turn the shell tote right-side out and place it inside the lining (still wrong-side out) so that the right sides are together, matching all seams and raw edges. Fold the handles back, out of the way, and tuck them between the shell and lining, then pin the upper raw edges together. Sew the shell and lining together around the top edge.

14 Reach through the opening and grasp the shell to turn the tote right-side out. Slip-stitch the gap in the lining seam by hand, or press the seam allowances to the wrong side along the opening, lay the folds on top of one another, and stitch by machine. Arrange the lining inside the tote shell so it fits snugly. Press the top edge flat. Smooth the

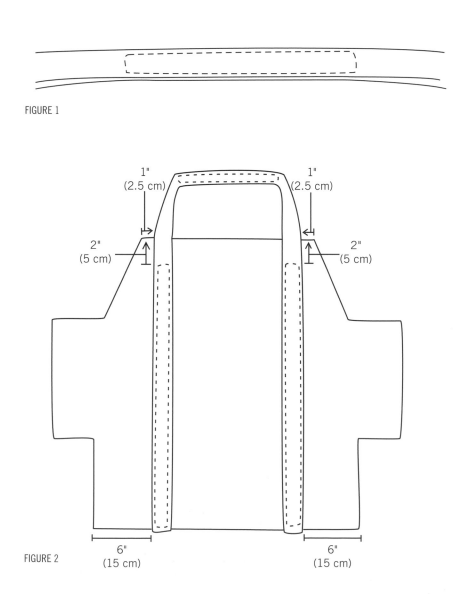

FIGURE 1

1" (2.5 cm) 1" (2.5 cm)

2" (5 cm) 2" (5 cm)

FIGURE 2

6" (15 cm) 6" (15 cm)

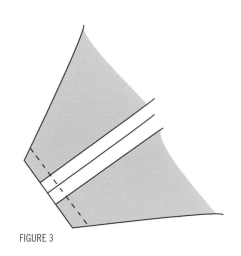

FIGURE 3

handles into place, extending past the carrier's upper edge, and pin the handles to the shell. Starting at one side seam, topstitch around the tote's upper edge, ¼" (6 mm) from the seam, topstitching across the handles to hold them in place.

15 Measure and mark the upper edge 6" (15 cm) from the side seams on both the carrier front and back.

16 Fold the carrier, lining sides together, parallel to the side seam, folding from the mark on the upper edge to the end of the boxing seam from Step 11, press to crease. Topstitch ¼" (6 mm) from the fold, backtacking at both ends; this creates a tuck. Repeat at the other three marks from Step 15 to define the carrier sides. 🍃

ERIN HARRIS blogs about her crafting adventures at houseonhillroad.com.

Firewood Tote
body
cut 4 on fold

place on fold

Enlarge template 400%

sdie edge

bottom edge

Artful Eco Bags

by Kelli Perkins

In the past year, we've all become more aware of the impact of plastic grocery bags on the environment. The kindest thing we can do is to replace them with a reusable alternative. Why not make a boodle of fabric replacement bags, customized for your recipient? Everyone from moms to students can appreciate these little bags, with lots of room for groceries, library books, or art supplies. You can whip them up in no time, so plan to make a few for yourself as well. The best part is that you can roll them up and tuck them into your purse or glove box, so they're always handy for impromptu market strolls. If they get soiled, pop them in the washing machine and they're ready for the next trip.

Materials
—1 yd (91.5 cm) printed cotton fabric

—24" (61 cm) matching grosgrain ribbon

—Machine thread

—Template on page 42

Optional
—Plain canvas

—Fabric paint and paintbrush, if you want to paint, stamp, or stencil your own designs onto your bag

Directions

1 Cut 2 each of bag body and facing.

2 Turn under ¼" (6 mm) along the long bottom edge of a facing piece 2 times and zigzag stitch to finish it. Repeat with the other facing.

3 Place a bag body and facing right sides together and pin in place. Using a ½" (1.3 cm) seam, stitch around the bag top, from side seam to side seam (but not sewing the side seams), leaving the very top of each handle open. Repeat with the other bag body and facing. Clip all curves and turn each piece right-side out, then iron.

4 Fold the ribbon in half, locate the center of one bag side, and pin the ribbon to the bag body (fabric right-side up) so that the long pieces are toward the center of the bag and the folded edge aligns with the raw edge.

5 Place 2 bag bodies right sides together with the facing flipped up and pin. Stitch around the entire perimeter of the bag, from the edge of the facing piece, down the side, bottom, other side, and through to the end of the other side facing.

6 Make a gusset in each bottom corner by aligning the bottom seam with a side seam and opening the seam allowances flat. Sew straight across the corner about 1½" (3.8 cm) in from the tip. Repeat for the second

gusset. Zigzag stitch the interior seam allowances to finish. Turn the bag right-side out and press.

7 Secure the facing to the inside by stitching down each side seam from the top of the bag to the end of the facing, using a zigzag stitch and coordinating thread.

8 With the bag turned right-side out and the facing on the inside, sew straight across each pair of handles, 1½" (3.8 cm) down from the top. Trim one of the 1½" (3.8 cm) flaps to ¼" (6 mm), and fold the raw edge. Fold the raw edge of the other flap under ¼" (6 mm), and pin it over the trimmed edge. Topstitch around the created rectangle.

9 To add letter blocks, cut some pieces of plain cotton canvas to whatever size you'd like. With black fabric paint, stamp block letters onto the canvas, then highlight them with a coordinating color of paint in

a random stipple. Allow the paint to dry and then iron to set.

10 Dab the letters with a glue stick to temporarily hold them in place while you position them. When you're satisfied, zigzag stitch around the canvas to attach the fabric blocks. With a coordinating color of thread, free-motion stitch around each stamped letter.

11 To roll up a bag, lay it out on a table, text-side up. Fold the handles down, fold the top down, and then fold the bottom up so that the ribbon is centered on the side. On the side opposite the ribbon, begin rolling up the bag jelly roll style and then tie it with the ribbon. 🍃

KELLI PERKINS shares her artistic journey through her blog at ephemeralalchemy.blogspot.com.

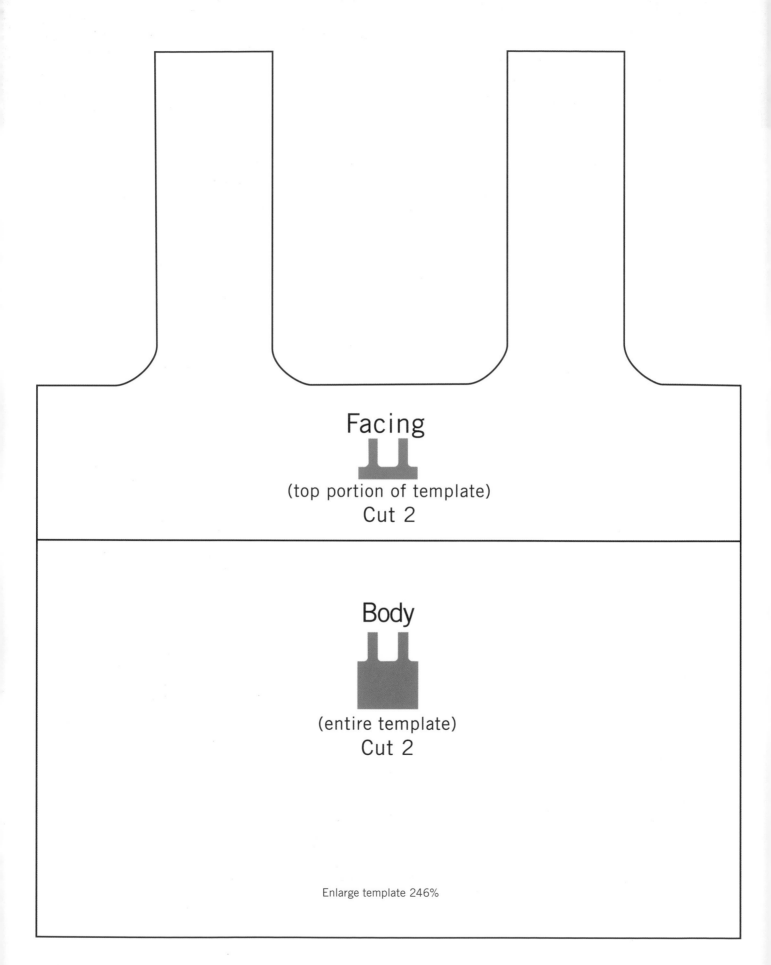

Facing

(top portion of template)

Cut 2

Body

(entire template)

Cut 2

Enlarge template 246%

Sewing Basics

A quick reference guide to basic tools, techniques, and terms

For the projects in this issue (unless otherwise indicated):

* When piecing: Use ¼" (6 mm) seam allowances. Stitch with the right sides together. After stitching a seam, press it to set the seam; then open the fabrics and press the seam allowance toward the darker fabric.

* Yardages are based upon 44" (112 cm) wide fabric.

Sewing Kit

The following items are essential for your sewing kit. Make sure you have these tools on hand before starting any of the projects:

* **ACRYLIC RULER** This is a clear flat ruler, with a measuring grid at least 2" × 18" (5 × 45.5 cm). A rigid acrylic (quilter's) ruler should be used when working with a rotary cutter. You should have a variety of rulers in different shapes and sizes.

* **BATTING** 100% cotton, 100% wool, plus bamboo, silk, and blends.

* **BONE FOLDER** Allows you to make non-permanent creases in fabric, paper, and other materials.

* **CRAFT SCISSORS** To use when cutting out paper patterns.

* **EMBROIDERY SCISSORS** These small scissors are used to trim off threads, clip corners, and do other intricate cutting work.

* **FABRIC** Commercial prints, hand-dyes, cottons, upholstery, silks, wools; the greater the variety of types, colors, designs, and textures, the better.

* **FABRIC MARKING PENS/PENCILS + TAILOR'S CHALK** Available in several colors for use on light and dark fabrics; use to trace patterns and pattern markings onto your fabric. Tailor's chalk is available in triangular pieces, rollers, and pencils. Some forms (such as powdered) can simply be brushed away; refer to the manufacturer's instructions for the recommended removal method for your chosen marking tool.

* **FREE-MOTION OR DARNING FOOT** Used to free-motion quilt.

* **FUSIBLE WEB** Used to fuse fabrics together. There are a variety of products on the market.

* **GLUE** Glue stick, fabric glue, and all-purpose glue.

* **HANDSEWING + EMBROIDERY NEEDLES** Keep an assortment of sewing and embroidery needles in different sizes, from fine to sturdy.

* **IRON, IRONING BOARD + PRESS CLOTHS** An iron is an essential tool when sewing. Use cotton muslin or silk organza as a press cloth to protect delicate fabric surfaces from direct heat. Use a Teflon sheet or parchment paper to protect your iron and ironing board when working with fusible web.

* **MEASURING TAPE** Make sure it's at least 60" (152.5 cm) long and retractable.

* **NEEDLE THREADER** An inexpensive aid to make threading the eye of the needle super fast.

* **PINKING SHEARS** These scissors with notched teeth leave a zigzag edge on the cut cloth to prevent fraying.

* **POINT TURNER** A blunt, pointed tool that helps push out the corners of a project and/or smooth seams. A knitting needle or chopstick may also be used.

* **ROTARY CUTTER + SELF-HEALING MAT** Useful for cutting out fabric quickly. Always use a mat to protect the blade and your work surface (a rigid acrylic ruler should be used with a rotary cutter to make straight cuts).

* **SAFTEY PINS** Always have a bunch on hand.

* **SCISSORS** Heavy-duty shears reserved for fabric only; a pair of small, sharp embroidery scissors; thread snips; a pair of all-purpose scissors; pinking shears.

* **SEAM RIPPER** Handy for quickly ripping out stitches.

* **SEWING MACHINE** With free-motion capabilities.

* **STRAIGHT PINS + PINCUSHION** Always keep lots of pins nearby.

* **TEMPLATE SUPPLIES** Keep freezer paper or other large paper (such as parchment paper) on hand for tracing the templates you intend to use. Regular office paper may be used for templates that will fit. You should also have card stock or plastic if you wish to make permanent templates that can be reused.

* **THIMBLE** Your fingers and thumbs will thank you.

* **THREAD** All types, including hand and machine thread for stitching and quilting; variegated; metallic; 100% cotton; monofilament.

* **ZIPPER FOOT** An accessory foot for your machine with a narrow profile that can be positioned to sew close to the zipper teeth. A zipper foot is adjustable so the foot can be moved to either side of the needle.

Glossary of Sewing Terms and Techniques

BACKSTITCH Stitching in reverse for a short distance at the beginning and end of a seam line to secure the stitches. Most machines have a button or knob for this function (also called backtack).

BASTING Using long, loose stitches to hold something in place temporarily. To baste by machine, use the longest straight stitch length available on your machine. To baste by hand, use stitches at least ¼" (6 mm) long. Use a contrasting thread to make the stitches easier to spot for removal.

BIAS The direction across a fabric that is located at a 45-degree angle from the lengthwise or crosswise grain. The bias has high stretch and a very fluid drape.

BIAS TAPE Made from fabric strips cut on a 45-degree angle to the grainline, the bias cut creates an edging fabric that will stretch to enclose smooth or curved edges. You can buy bias tape ready-made or make your own.

CLIPPING CURVES Involves cutting tiny slits or triangles into the seam allowance of curved edges so the seam will lie flat when turned right-side out. Cut slits along concave curves and triangles (with points toward the seam line) along a convex curve. Be careful not to clip into the stitches.

CLIP THE CORNERS Clipping the corners of a project reduces bulk and allows for crisper corners in the finished project. To clip a corner, cut off a triangle-shaped piece of fabric across the seam allowances at the corner. Cut close to the seam line but be careful not to cut through the stitches.

DART This stitched triangular fold is used to give shape and form to the fabric to fit body curves.

EDGESTITCH A row of topstitching placed very close (1⁄16"–1⁄8" [2–3 mm]) to an edge or an existing seam line.

FABRIC GRAIN The grain is created in a woven fabric by the threads that travel lengthwise and crosswise. The lengthwise grain runs parallel to the selvedges; the crosswise grain should always be perpendicular to the lengthwise threads. If the grains aren't completely straight and perpendicular, grasp the fabric at diagonally opposite corners and pull gently to restore the grain. In knit fabrics, the lengthwise grain runs along the wales (ribs), parallel to the selvedges, with the crosswise grain running along the courses (perpendicular to the wales).

FINGER-PRESS Pressing a fold or crease with your fingers as opposed to using an iron.

FUSSY-CUT Cutting a specific motif from a commercial or hand-printed fabric. Generally used to center a motif in a patchwork pattern or to feature a specific motif in an appliqué design. Use a clear acrylic ruler or template plastic to isolate the selected motif and ensure that it will fit within the desired size, including seam allowances.

GRAINLINE A pattern marking showing the direction of the grain. Make sure the grainline marked on the pattern runs parallel to the lengthwise grain of your fabric, unless the grainline is specifically marked as crosswise or bias.

INTERFACING Material used to stabilize or reinforce fabrics. Fusible interfacing has an adhesive coating on one side that adheres to fabric when ironed.

LINING The inner fabric of a garment or bag, used to create a finished interior that covers the raw edges of the seams.

MITER Joining a seam or fold at an angle that bisects the project corner. Most common is a 45-degree angle, like a picture frame, but shapes other than squares or rectangles will have miters with different angles.

OVERCAST STITCH A machine stitch that wraps around the fabric raw edge to finish edges and prevent unraveling. Some sewing machines have several overcast stitch options; consult your sewing machine manual for information on stitch settings and the appropriate presser foot for the chosen stitch (often the standard presser foot can be used). A zigzag stitch can be used as an alternative to finish raw edges if your machine doesn't have an overcast stitch function.

PRESHRINK Many fabrics shrink when washed; you need to wash, dry, and press all your fabric before you start to sew, following the suggested cleaning method marked on the fabric bolt (keep in mind that the appropriate cleaning method may not be machine washing). Don't skip this step!

RIGHT SIDE The front side, or the side that should be on the outside of a finished garment. On a print fabric, the print will be stronger on the right side of the fabric.

RIGHT SIDES TOGETHER The right sides of two fabric layers should be facing each other.

SATIN STITCH (MACHINE) This is a smooth, completely filled column of zigzag stitches achieved by setting the stitch length short enough for complete coverage but long enough to prevent bunching and thread buildup.

SEAM ALLOWANCE The amount of fabric between the raw edge and the seam.

SELVEDGE This is the tightly woven border on the lengthwise edges of woven fabric and the finished lengthwise edges of knit fabric.

SQUARING UP After you have pieced together a fabric block or section, check to make sure the edges are straight and the measurements are correct. Use a rotary cutter and an acrylic ruler to trim the block if necessary.

STITCH IN THE DITCH Lay the quilt sandwich right-side up under the presser foot and sew along the seam line "ditch." The stitches will fall between the two fabric pieces and disappear into the seam.

TOPSTITCH Used to hold pieces firmly in place and/or to add a decorative effect, a topstitch is simply a stitch that can be seen on the outside of the garment or piece. To topstitch, make a line of stitching on the outside (right side) of the piece, usually a set distance from an existing seam.

UNDERSTITCHING A line of stitches placed on a facing (or lining), very near the facing/garment seam. Understitching is used to hold the seam allowances and facing together and to prevent the facing from rolling toward the outside of the garment.

WRONG SIDE The wrong side of the fabric is the underside, or the side that should be on the inside of a finished garment. On a print fabric, the print will be lighter or less obvious on the wrong side of the fabric.

Stitch Glossary

Backstitch

Working from right to left, bring the needle up at **1** and insert behind the starting point at **2**. Bring the needle up at **3**, repeat by inserting at **1** and bringing the needle up at a point that is a stitch length beyond **3**.

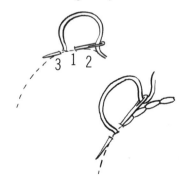

Basting Stitch

Using the longest straight stitch length on your machine, baste to temporarily hold fabric layers and seams in position for final stitching. It can also be done by hand. When basting, use a contrasting thread to make it easier to spot when you're taking it out.

Blanket Stitch

Working from left to right, bring the needle up at **1** and insert at **2**. Bring the needle back up at **3** and over the working thread. Repeat by making the next stitch in the same manner, keeping the spacing even.

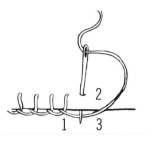

Blindstitch/Blind-Hem Stitch

Used mainly for hemming fabrics where an inconspicuous hem is difficult to achieve (this stitch is also useful for securing binding on the wrong side). Fold the hem edge back about ¼" (6 mm). Take a small stitch in the garment, picking up only a few threads of the fabric, then take the next stitch ¼" (6 mm) ahead in the hem. Continue, alternating stitches between the hem and the garment (if using for a non-hemming application, simply alternate stitches between the two fabric edges being joined).

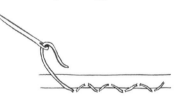

Chain Stitch

Working from top to bottom, bring the needle up at and reinsert at **1** to create a loop; do not pull the thread taut. Bring the needle back up at **2**, keeping the needle above the loop and gently pulling the needle toward you to tighten the loop flush to the fabric.

Repeat by inserting the needle at **2** to form a loop and bring the needle up at **3**. Tack the last loop down with a straight stitch.

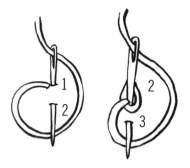

Straight Stitch + Running Stitch

Working from right to left, make a straight stitch by bringing the needle up and insert at **1**, ⅛"–¼" (3–6 mm) from the starting point. To make a line of running stitches (a row of straight stitches worked one after the other), bring the needle up at **2** and repeat.

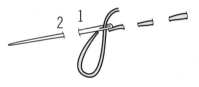

French Knot

Bring the needle up at **1** and hold the thread taut above the fabric. Point the needle toward your fingers and move the needle in a circular motion to wrap the thread around the needle once or twice. Insert the needle near **1** and hold the thread taut near the knot as you pull the needle and thread through the knot and the fabric to complete.

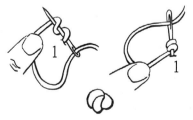

Couching

Working from right to left, use one thread, known as the couching or working thread, to tack down one or more strands of fiber, known as the couched fibers. Bring the working thread up at **1** and insert at **2**, over the fibers to tack them down, bringing the needle back up at **3**. The fibers are now encircled by the couching thread. Repeat to couch the desired length of fiber(s). This stitch may also be worked from left to right, and the spacing between the couching threads may vary for different design effects.

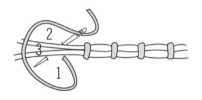

Cross-Stitch

Working from right to left, bring the needle up at **1**, insert at **2**, then bring the needle back up at **3**. Finish by inserting the needle at **4**. Repeat for the desired number of stitches.

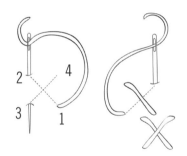

Whipstitch

Bring the needle up at **1**, insert at **2**, and bring up at **3**. These quick stitches do not have to be very tight or close together.

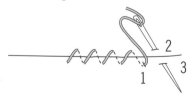

Standard Hand-Appliqué Stitch

Cut a length of thread 12"–18" (30.5–45.5 cm). Thread the newly cut end through the eye of the needle, pull this end through, and knot it. Use this technique to thread the needle and knot the thread to help keep the thread's "twist" intact and to reduce knotting. Beginning at the straightest edge of the appliqué and working from right to left, bring the needle up from the underside, through the background fabric and the very edge of the appliqué at **1**, catching only a few threads of the appliqué fabric. Pull the thread taut, then insert the needle into the background fabric at **2**, as close as possible to **1**. Bring the needle up through the background fabric at **3**, ⅛" (3 mm) beyond **2**. Continue in this manner, keeping the thread taut (do not pull it so tight that the fabric puckers) to keep the stitching as invisible as possible.

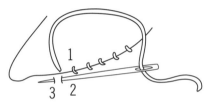

Slip Stitch

Working from right to left, join two pieces of fabric by taking a ¹⁄₁₆"–¼" (2–6 mm) long stitch into the folded edge of one piece of fabric and bringing the needle out. Insert the needle into the folded edge of the other piece of fabric, directly across from the point where the thread emerged from the previous stitch. Repeat by inserting the needle into the first piece of fabric. The thread will be almost entirely hidden inside the folds of the fabrics.

Create Binding
Cutting Straight Strips

Cut strips on the crosswise grain, from selvedge to selvedge. Use a rotary cutter and straightedge to obtain a straight cut. Remove the selvedges and join the strips with diagonal seams (see instructions at right).

Cutting Bias Strips

Fold one cut end of the fabric to meet one selvedge, forming a fold at a 45-degree angle to the selvedge (**1**). With the fabric placed on a self-healing mat, cut off the fold with a rotary cutter, using a straightedge as a guide to make a straight cut. With the straightedge and rotary cutter, cut strips to the appropriate width (**2**). Join the strips with diagonal seams.

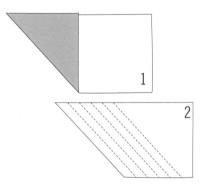

Binding with Mitered Corners

Decide whether you will use a Double-fold Binding (option A at right) or a Double-layer Binding (option B at right). *If using double-layer binding follow the alternate italicized instructions in parenthesis.*

Open the binding and press ½" (1.3 cm) to the wrong side at one short end *(refold the binding at the center crease and proceed)*. Starting with the folded-under end of the binding, place it near the center of the first edge of the project to be bound, matching the raw edges, and pin in place. Begin sewing near the center of one edge of the project, along the first crease *(at the appropriate distance from the raw edge)*, leaving several inches of the binding fabric free at the beginning. Stop sewing ¼" (6 mm) before reaching the corner, backstitch, and cut the threads. Rotate the project 90 degrees to position it for sewing the next side. Fold the binding fabric up, away from the project, at a 45-degree angle (**1**), then fold it back down along the project raw edge (**2**). This forms a miter at the corner. Stitch the second side, beginning at the project raw edge (**2**) and ending ¼" (6 mm) from the next corner, as before.

Continue as established until you have completed the last corner. Continue stitching until you are a few inches from the beginning edge of the binding fabric. Overlap the pressed beginning edge of the binding by ½" (1.3 cm) (or overlap more as necessary for security) and trim the working edge to fit. Finish sewing the binding (*opening the center fold and tucking the raw edge inside the pressed end of the binding strip*). Refold the binding along all the creases and then fold it over the project raw edges to the back, enclosing the raw edges (*there are no creases to worry about with option B*). The folded edge of the binding strip should just cover the stitches visible on the project back. Slip-stitch or blindstitch the binding in place, tucking in the corners to complete the miters as you go (**3**).

Diagonal Seams for Joining Strips
Lay two strips right sides together, at right angles. The area where the strips overlap forms a square. Sew diagonally across the square as shown above. Trim the excess fabric ¼" (6 mm) away from the seam line and press the seam allowances open. Repeat to join all the strips, forming one long fabric band.

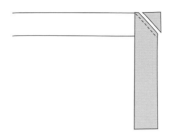

Fold Binding
A. Double-fold Binding
This option will create binding that is similar to packaged double-fold bias tape/binding. Fold the strip in half lengthwise, with wrong sides together; press. Open up the fold and then fold each long edge toward the wrong side, so that the raw edges meet in the middle (**1**). Refold the binding along the existing center crease, enclosing the raw edges (**2**), and press again.

B. Double-layer Binding
This option creates a double-thick binding with only one fold. This binding is often favored by quilters. Fold the strip in half lengthwise with wrong sides together; press.

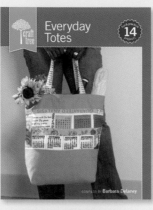